NELLA

A PSYCHIC EYE

NELLA

A PSYCHIC EYE

How to see into the Mind, the Future and the World Beyond

Nella Jones
with
Mandy Bruce

EBURY PRESS
LONDON

Published in 1992 by Ebury Press
an imprint of Random House UK Ltd
Random House
20 Vauxhall Bridge Road
London SW1V 2SA

Catalogue record for this book is available
from the British Library.

ISBN 0 09 177242 7

Editor: Susan Baker
Designer: Oliver Hickey

Typeset in Plantin by Hope Services (Abingdon) Ltd.
and bound in Great Britain
by Mackays of Chatham PLC, Chatham, Kent

Contents

For Jacob

Acknowledgements

I would like to thank the many people who have helped with this book for their time, support and encouragement. Many thanks to all my friends in the police force, especially Detective Constable Neil Pratt, Detective Inspector Don Middleton and Chief Inspector Dave Morgan. Also Tony Dunn, Dr Wedderspoon, Mavis, Ross Tayne, Susan Druckman and Carole Garside, not just for the typing but for her great enthusiasm. Special thanks to Gaynor and Karl and my dear friends Pat, Mavis, Toots and Lou.

ONE

Beginnings

Who Am I?

I'm a friend to a lonely stranger,
I'm the mother that calms your fears,
I'm the mistress to the businessman,
I'm the nurse that can dry your tears.

I'm the sister to the brother,
I'm the wife of a happy man,
Whatever you want in a woman
That is what I am.

NELLA JONES,
1991

I was only seven years old when I started to get the lonely feeling. A wiry slip of a thing I was then. A little girl with long brown hair and skinny legs, all wrapped up in one of my sister's hand-me-down coats with sleeves too long for me. A little girl with a secret, a strange feeling that the world I saw all around me was not quite as it seemed.

In many ways it was a desperate time. The war had just begun and you could almost touch the worry that hung in the air. We were very poor and I remember sometimes being so hungry that my brother James and I would sneak into a farmer's field, dig up a cabbage and munch it so fast that we invariably had indigestion by the time we got home to Number Three Church Cottages.

I loved Number Three Church Cottages. Open the door and you could walk straight into the cosy front room and, if you looked through to the kitchen, you could see our big, old-fashioned iron range.

And I loved Eynsford, our village. They call Kent the 'Garden of England' and Eynsford is still one of its prettiest pockets. There wasn't much to it in those days: one main road, the High Street, with tumble-down houses and shops lined up on either side, a church, a bridge.

To seven-year-old me, it was a truly magical place. In winter, when it snowed hard, it looked like a living Christmas card; so beautiful that sometimes I was afraid to walk in the snow in case I spoiled the beautiful picture I was living in.

In summer you could actually smell the green of the countryside, and the highlight of the summer holidays was the sports day the village held every year.

The locals used to call me Sunshine because I was always laughing, always smiling – and I was the fastest kid on the block.

I could run like the wind. They gave prizes of money and Mr Hoy, who owned the local factory, kept records. Kids from all the surrounding villages turned up to join in the races but I would take off my shoes and run barefoot and nothing on two legs could catch me.

In the village I used to run errands for everyone. They would say, 'Nell, she'll go for you,' and I would run down to the local shops and then run back and take messages here, there and everywhere.

There was one dear old lady who lived in Rose Cottage and I always used to stop and talk to her. She looked very old to me, small and hunched, and she always wore a pinny over her frock. She would stand by her gate and tell me she was waiting for her son who had gone away to war.

I used to think, 'Isn't it sad, she is waiting there for him and he isn't going to come back because he's dead.' I don't know how I knew that, I just knew. And I knew I couldn't tell her because she would be so upset.

One day after I had seen her I felt an overwhelming sadness.

'What's the matter with you?' asked my friend Barbara.

'It's that poor old lady – she's going to die.'

'Don't be silly,' she said, and we forgot all about it – until a week later the old lady died. I wasn't surprised. I knew she was going to die and it made me sad because she was a lovely old soul. But after that, when I was running errands in the village, I found that none of the children would talk to me. I went and found Barbara. She tried to avoid me but I chased her down the lane and got her by the scruff of the neck.

I was so upset. 'Why aren't you lot talking to me any more?'

She screeched at me, 'Because you're a witch! You said the old lady was going to die, you made her die! My Mum said I'm not to play with you because you're a witch!' And she ran off.

After that it happened more often. Sometimes I would feel compelled to go somewhere. I would walk out of the lane and into a field and always I would meet someone or find something. Once, for no reason at all, my feet wouldn't let me pass a gate which opened into a lonely copse. So I went through the gate and, down in a pit, I found a pure white handkerchief, folded into four, and on top of it was a gold watch, a comb and some money. It was a real treasure trove!

Sometimes I would say things without thinking, things I just felt compelled to say.

I found a big, old, rusty nail one day and every evening I went down to the bridge and scratched away at the stone parapet. I did that for weeks and weeks until I had managed to etch my initials, really deeply into the bridge, N. S. – Nella Saunders.

When I finally finished I had two friends with me – Arthur, a boy from the next village of Farningham, and Edna, a red-haired girl who lived up School Lane. I turned to them and said, 'When these initials fade off this bridge, I will die.'

They looked at me as if I was mad and that is when I got the lonely feeling so strongly. They didn't know why I said these things and I didn't either. I was still Sunshine. I still kept laughing and smiling, but there was an ache inside myself, a deep-down feeling that I was changing.

I began to realise that there was something very different about me. I knew it was an absolute waste of time trying to make anybody understand, so I had to keep it to myself.

I still get the lonely feeling. I feel it well up inside me. It comes and goes. I get it whenever I am helping the police to look for a murderer, and I feel I am getting close to him. And when I feel the full force of an evil murderer's mind, the Yorkshire Ripper for example, the feeling can be overwhelming.

When people do not like what I have said I get it. Earlier this year I was asked by a newspaper to contact the dead tycoon Robert Maxwell on the other side, and when they published some of the things he told me, I received death threats over the phone from people who claimed to be friends of his. The police had to intercept my calls in the end, but at the time, when I was standing there holding the phone, it was not just fear I was feeling, it was loneliness.

Growing up in Eynsford was the beginning of the lonely feeling but, looking back, it was not the beginning of being different, being *psychic*. I suppose it was just that, before Eynsford, I thought everybody saw the spirits I saw, and everybody else could see into the future just as I could.

I was born in early summer, on the fourth of May, 1932, in a tin shack on Belvedere marshes in Kent. My mother, Edith, was a tiny little thing and timid, too, although she had a terrible temper on her when she was riled. She was a Romany gypsy and came from good fairground stock. Her father used to be a fairground boxer and her mother used to make the toffee apples and rock candy they sold at the fair.

My father, Herbert, was a bully. He was a big man, broad and tall, with big hands. His father had been an architect but I never met that side of the family.

There were six of us children – Albert, Elizabeth, Daisy, James, me and, a few years later, my sister Margaret came along. So I was number five, although my Mum lost two babies, so I should have been number seven. My father called me Nelly but Mum, and everyone else since, has always called me Nell.

I don't remember the shack. My earliest memories are of the gypsy encampment we moved to afterwards. There were always lots of people around, some gypsy families and some who were not gypsies at all. It was 1935, a time of recession, and everyone was scratching around making a living any way they could. It was hard for us, too. The older kids used to look after me while Mum went off to work. She was doing everything she could to earn the money to keep us and I still remember sitting outside our caravan waiting for her to come home in the evenings.

Then Mum and Dad got jobs working on a farm, planting in the fields and digging potatoes, and we moved into a lovely thatched house called Home Farm. And that is where I first met the spirit children.

Three of us girls used to sleep together in one big bed and when my older sisters had fallen asleep, there were three children who used to visit me. When they came into the room they didn't walk through the door; somehow they were just suddenly there! And when they left, they didn't go out of the door or the window or walk through the walls – they would just suddenly be gone.

The mysterious children were a girl of about ten, a boy who must have been about nine and another little girl who was about six – a year older than me.

They did not tell me who they were and it did not seem to matter. We were just kids happy to be together. I loved seeing them. Every night, tucked up under the covers in my long winceyette nightie, I would stay awake hoping they would visit.

The girls wore funny boots on their feet, with lots of buttons, and I loved their dresses which came right down to just above their ankles

4

and which they covered with pretty pinafores. They used to laugh and squabble among themselves and they would talk to me and say, 'Hello Nella, what have you done today?'

One night, I proudly told the little boy about the pennies I had put in the bank. I felt really rich because I had found two pennies and I had heard the grown-ups talking about putting money in the bank, so I said to Mum, 'I'm going to put these pennies in the bank,' and she said it was a very good thing to do, to save money. So, the next day, I went out into the fields, found a grassy bank, dug a hole and hid the pennies.

I told the children all about it but the boy was not impressed. 'That's a bit stupid,' he said, 'you'll never find them again.' I was pretty upset by that and the next morning I went looking for them. But he was right, I couldn't find them anywhere.

I didn't tell my sisters about the children. I didn't tell a soul, but all the family knew that the house was haunted. Sometimes, when everybody was in bed at night, we would hear the latches on the doors lift up. Then, one by one, the doors would open and there would be footsteps on the stairs.

It was just something we accepted; we had to put up with it. Sometimes the rest of the family got scared, but I wasn't frightened. It never bothered me one little bit. It seemed totally normal to me that doors would open of their own accord. They always had.

I saw the children right up until the time we left that house and I was sorry to say goodbye to them. We had been friends for nearly three years, a long time when you are a child.

The next house we moved to was haunted too – every house I have ever lived in seems to have been haunted – but it was not the same. At Mussenden Cottages, in Mussenden Lane, the whole family would hear a coach and horses driving fast down the lane, but when we looked out there was never anyone there.

It was a bad time for the family. My father was a violent man. He did not drink much so it was not drink that was to blame. He would just go mad. Then he would thump Mum and the kids, including me. One night he tried to set fire to the house with us in it and then he beat Mum black and blue. He tried to choke her, in fact he nearly choked the life out of her, and she knew she had to leave him. She had nowhere to go, so she couldn't take us with her. But I never blamed her for that. She knew the older ones would look after the little ones.

At night, after she had gone, I remember lying in bed with my sisters looking at the little window next to us. It was fascinating. As I watched, the latch would lift up and the window would open all on its own. I wasn't scared. I just used to think, 'Well, isn't that funny.'

Then one night, about three months after Mum had left, I turned over and I saw a lady standing by the bed. I could see her so clearly. She had grey hair, parted in the middle, and pulled back in a kind of bun. She was wearing a long grey nightdress and she must have been in her forties.

I can see her in my mind now, although it makes me cry to think of her because in my child's mind I thought it was Mum. I know, looking back, she didn't look anything like Mum but I said, 'Hello Mum, when did you come back?' But she said nothing. She just smiled at me and she was gone as swiftly as she had appeared.

In the morning I rushed into Dad's bedroom and asked, 'Where's Mum then?'

He replied, 'What are you talking about?'

Even now I can feel the disappointment. It was not until years later when my sister, Lizzie, came to visit, and we were talking about old times, that she told me she had seen the lady, too. But we never told each other and now I wish we had.

As kids we didn't realise how terrifying the war was. We'd watch the Spitfires and the German aircraft fighting out the Battle of Britain in the sky above us and it was exciting. But one day, when a Luftwaffe plane flew low and machine-gunned us, we had to jump into a ditch: we were frightened to death.

Dad wasn't called-up because he was working at Vickers, the armament factory in Crayford, but my brother Albert was in the Home Guard and he used to tell us how he had to go to the site of plane crashes and pick up boots with feet in them and gloves with hands in them.

After a while, I think we young ones became too much for Dad to cope with and he said that Margaret and I should go and live with our mother. She had set up home with a really nice man called Joe and the four of us moved into Church Cottages when he got a job on a farm in Eynsford.

I was still occasionally 'seeing' people. I would look up and see someone when no one else seemed to see them, but they were all quite friendly, so it didn't bother me. When Joe went into the army, I would say to my mother, 'Joe will be home next week,' and she would say, 'Don't be silly, you know he won't be home for three months.' But then he'd turn up and Mum would give me what we used to call an old-fashioned look!

After the old lady from Rose Cottage died, my friends used to think I was different from the rest of them. I did not want to be different at all; I wanted to be just like they were, but I could understand what they meant. Yet, they still flocked around me. If I was at the recreation ground, they would all come over and group around me. Somehow, people have always made me a centre of attention.

As I got older, lots of strange things began to happen. One night Mum and Joe went off to the pub for a drink and left me to look after my little sister who was asleep on the sofa. I was just sitting there and the brass plate on the wall caught my eye and I thought to myself, 'That's moving.'

As I looked at the plate, I could see a moving picture inside it. The colours were clear and vivid and the picture kept changing. It was like watching television today.

I could see a beautiful woman wearing a glowing, chiffon dress and she was in a perfect country garden. She carried a pitcher of water and she walked through the garden and sat down by a well. It was stunning and I sat there totally entranced by the picture until, after a while, it faded and the brass plate was a plate again.

Another night they went out and before she left I said to Mum, 'What shall I say to the photographer when he calls?'

She had ordered some photos he had taken of my sister and she said, 'Don't be silly, he's not coming for three weeks.'

I kept on, 'But he's coming tonight.' And, of course, he did.

I opened the door and there he was and, immediately, I had the feeling that the man was somehow dangerous. He wanted to come in but I would not let him. I told him, 'You'll have to come back in three weeks,' and slammed the door in his face.

My instincts about people have always been accurate. Sometimes I hear voices warning me and they've saved me from danger quite a few times. Once, my Mum sent my brother James and I off to buy some candles. It was a winter's evening, misty and foggy and getting dark and the dirt road was flanked by orchards on either side. It was a bit scary and quite a way to old Mr Elliott's, the first house along the track.

We were walking along, and mucking about like kids do, and suddenly I saw a man come out onto the road. There was nothing strange about that. Lots of the men in the district finished work at dusk, but I knew *he* was a threat to us. I knew it.

'Here comes a monster out of the dark,' said James. And I said, 'Yes, run, run!' He thought I had gone mad but I kept screaming at him to run, so he did. We just flew but, as we got level with the man, he tried to grab my brother and he latched on to the belt of my brother's coat. James managed to get free and we flew like the wind until we reached the Elliotts' house. The men there got the farmer's guns and went out looking for the strange man but they never caught up with him.

Another time, we were skipping down the lane when in the hedge there sat a strange old woman dressed completely in black. She said to me, 'Go on, my daughter, run, run like the wind,' so I did. James did not see her but I did and I trusted what she said to me. I just know she saved me from some sort of danger.

As I grew older I became more clairvoyant. I would somehow know when someone was going to die, but it wasn't just death I saw. Sometimes it was little everyday things. The first time it happened I was on the village bridge and a boy passed me. His father owned one of the big pubs and the lad had a really posh bike. He cycled so fast I had to jump into an alcove on the bridge to avoid getting mown down.

Without thinking I shouted after him, 'You'll be sorry, you're going to fall off that bike and you're going to hurt yourself,' and the next minute he did. He was furious and came back and told me I was a witch. But I was getting used to that!

Another time, there was a posh young lady in the village playing with her dog and a ball. I told her not to let the dog play with the ball because I knew it would be hurt. But she said, 'Mind your own business, gypsy,' and carried on playing. The ball was very soft and hollow. The dog opened its mouth wide, swallowed it and choked to death.

My mother often scolded me for being silly when I told her things that were going to happen. Sometimes she would say to me, 'Who told you that? Someone told you that, didn't they?' Then I'd say no one had told me but she would wallop me anyway.

Yet despite all that, I think that of all the people I knew when I was growing up, Mum was the one who most understood my gift. Maybe it worried her.

Later, when we were forced to move and live in an old bus, Mum used to have a fire burning outside during the summer where she boiled water and cooked. In the field, just beyond us, they had put up practice hurdles for the foxhunting horses. One day a very grand lady rode past. She had a whip and she kept smacking her shiny leather boot with it. She started having a go at Mum.

'How dare you build fires where horses have to pass,' she was shouting.

She was an odious woman, talking down to us because we were gypsies, and I found myself shouting back at her, 'I hope you fall off your horse and break your neck!'

She rode off into the field, fell at the first jump and broke her collar bone. I don't think I have ever seen Mum so angry.

I had meant what I said. At that moment I had hated that woman and I meant every word of it. It was the first time I had ever performed a curse and Mum got me by the scruff of the neck and hit me, yelling, 'Don't you ever wish bad on people again! You of all people!'

She knew. Even though she never talked to me about my gift, she knew. And I'm sure she had the gift herself. She chose not to use it but if she said something was going to happen you could bet your life it would.

We had to move out of Number Three Church Cottages because Joe lost his job and the house went with the job. For us, it was a disaster. My younger sister went to live with my older sister but Mum, Joe and I were left with nowhere to go and we ended up sleeping in an old Anderson shelter that someone had dug out during the war.

It was one of the worst times of my life. A young girl shouldn't have to live under ground. The shelter was so small that Mum and Joe used to take turns sleeping on a row of boxes by one wall.

I left school at 14 and every morning I would walk five miles along a lonely road to get to work at the Eynsford paper mills by seven o'clock. Then I would walk the five miles back again in the evening at about six. That was during the weekdays. All weekend I worked in a cafe. It was work, work, work but I didn't have any choice. We needed the money.

Joe got a job with a tree felling firm and I worked for them, too, for a while, until one frosty morning I had a nasty accident when I was swinging an axe and it slipped and cut me across the leg.

Shortly afterwards, the three of us were sitting in the shelter, an oil lamp on the table, listening to the radio when, suddenly, I screamed. I looked at Joe's hand and it was dripping with blood, there was blood everywhere.

I ran outside to get away from it and Joe followed me and Mum rushed out too. She couldn't understand what was the matter with me and all I could gasp was, 'Look at his hand! Look at his hand! It's bleeding!'

Joe tried to calm me down. 'But it's not bleeding, love.'

'It's just a trick of the light,' Mum said, 'It's nothing.' But I knew.

We moved out of the shelter and into the bus, which was a little better but not much. Then three weeks later Joe was late home from work. I could tell Mum was worried. She kept pacing up and down, watching out of the window anxiously every five minutes or so.

Hours later, the gaffer who ran the tree firm arrived. He said he was very sorry, but Joe was in Dartford Hospital. He had cut his hand badly on a saw. Mum looked at me and shook her head. I knew we were both thinking back to that night in the shelter but she didn't say a word.

While Joe was in hospital we struggled through a bad time. By now I wasn't just 'seeing things', I was sensing them all the time and it cut me off from everybody. I used to think, 'Who can I tell about this? How do I explain this to people?'

I used to meet people we knew and I would suddenly think: 'Oh dear, she's going to be very ill next week,' and I would want to tell someone – anyone – so much, but I couldn't.

The lonely feeling was stronger than ever. I couldn't see what was going to happen to me or to my mother, sisters and brothers. There were no sudden revelations about the family. Mostly, I would see things connected with people outside my own environment, people I did not know terribly well.

I now believe that whoever guides me, whatever spirit it is, must have thought, 'No, not the family. It would be too much for a child.' That is why, at that time, I could only see things outside my little world. But the feelings and sensations I had as a teenager were so extraordinary. Even if I lived to be a thousand, I could never fully explain them. They are beyond words.

I felt alone – but curiously, not alone. I have always known that there has been someone there, unseen, beside me the whole time. I promised my Mum I would never wish anything bad to happen to anyone again, and I have kept that promise. If anyone does anything really malicious to me I don't do anything to them. But always, throughout my life, I can guarantee that some disaster will happen to that person. It is not me doing it. I can say that with a clear conscience. But it always happens.

It is as if this spirit or lifeforce, or whoever it is that is with me, is making retribution on my behalf. Everyone who has ever tried a dirty rotten trick on me has come unstuck and, when bad things happen to them, I feel sorry – but it's not my doing.

The spirit who guides me is fantastically strong. I know it is male. He never showed himself to me as a child because I think he thought it would have been too much for me to take in and be at ease with. But now, as an adult, I see him quite often. He is not my earthly father but he calls me 'my child' and I call him 'my father'. But he is not God.

I can describe his 'physical' appearance to you. He is a spirit with a lovely face, thick white hair, a white beard and he looks very neat and tidy. Most of the time he wears what looks like a long shirt all the way down to the ground and it is tied in around his waist with a brown cord.

He wears brown sandals and they are done up with string and I feel he comes from a long time ago. But it is his eyes which affect me most. He has the most beautiful eyes I have ever seen, grey-green and so gentle. I see him as clearly as I can see anyone on this earth standing right in front of me. When I look into his eyes I gain great comfort and sometimes, when I've been crying, I look at him and I can see tears welling up in his eyes too. He is wisdom and he is always there for me. But even he hasn't stopped me from making fundamental mistakes in life.

I discovered love on a station platform when I was sixteen. I was a pretty girl in those days and boys had started showing an interest. There was one in particular – Albert – but it was nothing serious. If he had tried to hold my hand I would have run a mile! But this was the real thing.

Every week, I used to go to the pictures with a girlfriend in the nearest town for our weekly treat. One evening we were waiting on the platform to catch the train home to Eynsford when we saw this boy on the opposite platform walking up and down looking at me.

He came over the bridge and I thought, 'Oh blimey, what's this?' My friend and I were having a giggle about it and then he actually said those immortal words, 'Excuse me, do you come here often?' – which made us giggle even more.

I told him I was there every week because we went to the pictures and he said, 'If you're here next week I'll bring you a box of chocolates.' Well, everything was on rationing then, so I spent the whole week fantasising about the chocolates – and, of course, him!

The following week there he was, with the chocolates, and it was downhill all the way from then on.

His name was Eric and he was 24 – which is quite old as far as a sixteen-year-old girl is concerned. He was an electrician with his own business and I thought he was very sophisticated and superior. Quite a catch!

After the night of the chocolates, I saw him the following week, and the week after that, until I was going to the pictures every week with him instead of my girlfriend. We would say goodbye at the station. He offered me all the affection and attention I had never had. To him, there wasn't anything different about me, except that I was his special girl. With Eric I lost the lonely feeling. I thought the sun shone out of him, he was a dream come true, so when he suggested I go to London to live closer to him it did not take much persuading before I said yes.

I was very unhappy living in the bus, anyway. It wasn't just small and cramped, it was miserable. There was just Mum, Joe and I and Joe was not working because of the accident to his hand, so he was at home all day.

I did not tell Mum I was going because, if I had, she would never have let me go. She did not even know I had a boyfriend. So I just left, simply took off. At the age of 16 I disappeared.

Eric lived in Shepherd's Bush in West London and he helped me to find a room of my own in Acton, a mile or so up the road. Not surprisingly, that arrangement didn't last long. We decided to get married and we found a nice flat at 5, Bedford Street, in Fulham.

But first, because I was under age, we needed my parents' consent. I didn't want to ask Mum because I thought she was probably furious enough with me already. The problem was, I had not seen my father since I was a little girl at Home Farm.

So one day, for the first time, I decided to try and use my psychic gift to find him. Up until that moment I always felt I had no control over it. Things happened to me, I saw things, but never deliberately. Up until that time it had all happened at random. Now I was going to find out if my gift worked at *my* will.

I said to Eric, 'Come on, we're going to find Dad.' He thought I was daft.

'But you don't even know where he is,' he said. I had never told Eric that I was psychic. I never confided in him about all the strange things that had happened to me as I was growing up. I didn't want him to know, I didn't want him to think I was a witch, so I kept my trap shut.

Still, he agreed to come with me and we set off for the station.

For hours we got on trains and off trains, on buses and off buses. I just put all my faith in my instincts to get us where we had to go. I had the feeling that I had to go to Abbey Wood in Kent. I had not been there since I was a tiny child but now I knew that is where I had to go. When we finally reached the station my feet took me so deliberately in a certain direction, I felt as if I was merely following them.

I knew we had to get to a particular cafe. I had never been there before but I could see it in my mind and I knew that's where we had to go. My feet took me straight to it.

It was an ordinary sort of cafe; formica-topped tables were packed with workmen supping tea and smoking. Eric waited outside as I went in and had a look around. I saw a man sitting with his back to me at a table and I went up to him and tapped him on the shoulder.

'What the bloody hell do you want?' he muttered without even turning round.

'Hello Dad,' I said.

Then we were both in tears. Dad was crying, I was crying, in the end the whole cafe was crying! It was a lovely moment. He kept saying, 'But how the hell did you find me?' and there was nothing I could say except, 'I knew you were here,' and that was the truth.

Dad liked Eric on sight and, when we told him we wanted to get married, he was happy to sign the consent form. So, not long afterwards, we got married in the Baptist Church in Shepherd's Bush. I was a dream in cream! Cream blouse, skirt, and coat. I wore a beautiful cameo brooch but I didn't carry any flowers and none of my family were there.

In fact nobody came to my wedding and for me, in some ways, it was a sad day – because I was pregnant and because I knew the marriage wouldn't work or last. But, at the same time, I knew with an absolute certainty that I had to marry Eric because we were going to have two sons born very close together and I had to have those boys, they had to be born. Call it destiny if you like.

It was not long before things started to go wrong. There was no question of my sitting at home being a wife and mum. Eric made it quite clear that I had to work and I did – hard. I used to go out at four-thirty every morning and polish and scrub the doorsteps of the posh people's big houses in the area. Then, in the evenings I worked at the Empress Hall in Olympia as an usherette.

Everyone, including my father, thought Eric was whiter than white. I knew better. I thought he had an eye for the ladies. I didn't trust him. He would walk in the door and say he had been working late and I used to think, 'You lying sod.' I had my son, Eric, when I was seventeen and Peter was born one year and ten months later. The babies were beautiful and, like all new mums, I loved them with a passion. But they were the only bright lights in my life. I was miserable and on my own most of the time. I knew nobody in London and that is hard when you have two little ones and a wayward husband.

We started having rows and one night it got quite violent. I knew this was the moment to leave him and take the boys with me.

We owned the house in Bedford Road by then but there was no chance of forcing Eric to leave. In those days a house wasn't in joint names. If you had a house it belonged to the husband and if the wife left she didn't get a penny.

So I left that house with little Eric who was seven, Peter who was six, a small suitcase and just seven pound notes in my purse. I did not have a clue what we were going to do, so I set off for Abbey Wood where I knew my Dad was living on a caravan site.

He managed to get the landlord to rent us a little caravan and we moved in straight away. It was not exactly a palace but, as they say, it was home. I did my best to make it warm and comfortable and we kept it spotlessly clean. It was like a little box. There was a tiny solid fuel stove at one end, a chest of drawers, a table and one bed. The boys slept there and I slept on the floor.

Then I had to find a way of earning some money to keep the three of us. As I wandered aimlessly around Abbey Wood I saw totters going from door to door; women who would collect jumble and then sell it and I thought, 'Nell, if they can do it so can you'.

I put the boys into school and I borrowed a pram. Then, I went around all the local houses, asking for old clothes. I was only 24 and I spoke quite nicely because that was one thing Eric had always insisted on. So, some of the people gave me funny looks when I turned up on the doorstep with my pram and said in my proper voice, 'Excuse me, but do you have any old clothes you don't want?'

I was always back home in the afternoons in time to meet the boys when they came back from school and we would spend the evenings sorting out what I'd managed to acquire that day. The good clothing we put to one side, the wool to another, the rubbish that wasn't worth anything to another.

Maybe because I didn't seem like most people's idea of a gypsy I was given some good jumble, of a better quality than the other totters' haul, so they used to come and buy stuff from me. The rest I would take to a big factory down the road which bought rags and such like.

And that is how I kept the children and the family together. It wasn't ideal but, when you're broke, you can't afford to be proud, and it was honest work. The kids were happy and I kept them spotlessly clean, just like the caravan. They were enjoying school and I felt we were surviving quite well until a series of disasters changed our lives.

I came home early one day and went across the site to see Dad in his caravan. I went straight in but what I saw made me stop, rigid with shock. I felt sick. He was there naked with a thirteen-year-old girl. What happened next is a blur. We argued and he was so angry he lost his temper. He beat me up so badly they had to take me off to St Nicholas', the local hospital.

He said he was going to 'get me' because, I suppose, I had found out what he was up to. And he did. He got me good and proper. He hit me where it hurt most, he did the worst thing he could to me – thanks to him I lost my children.

I had not told my husband, Eric, where we were because I didn't want him coming after us, but while I was in hospital Dad rang him and said, 'You've got to come and get these children, they're living like gypsies.'

One Saturday when I had just done the washing, the boys were playing outside and a man came into the caravan and said he was from the welfare office.

He said, 'Mrs Jones?'

'Yes.'

'I've just come to see you and the children. They look very clean and well cared for.'

'Well, what did you expect?'

'You've made this place very cosy haven't you?' He looked almost guilty as he added, 'I'm very sorry about this.' I didn't know what he was talking about.

'Sorry about what?'

Then I looked outside. There was another man. He had grabbed the boys and was bundling them into a car while the other one kept me talking in the caravan. Dad had told Eric and Eric had complained to the authorities. I could see Eric sitting out there in the car watching what was happening. I could not believe it.

'I'm very sorry,' said the man in front of me, 'but your husband has got custody,' and he left.

I went berserk, I was so distraught. All I wanted was my children. And I wanted to kill Dad. I was going to kill him. I got an axe and I went to wait for him, but someone called the police and they arrived before he did. They asked me who I was waiting for. I remember saying, 'What's it to you – I'm not breaking the law.'

The police officer was a kind man. He seemed to understand and, eventually, he calmed me down, finally convincing me that killing Dad was not the answer and it was not worth getting myself into trouble. The weeks that followed were the bleakest of my life. I wandered around like a lost soul. I tried and tried to use my psychic gift to find out where the boys had been taken, but for the first time in my life, it let me down. The harder I tried, the less I could see. I found out Eric had sent them away to a boarding school but I didn't know where. I tried everything I could to get the boys back. I visited the local social services department only to find I was in a classic *Catch 22* situation. I asked for a council house so I could live with my children. They said I could only have one if the children are in my custody. But I couldn't get custody until I had a house.

Life seemed to have lost its meaning. I don't remember much about the first three months. It was a time of total despair. I never heard from Mum. Dad was down in his caravan and I was in mine but we never spoke and I never forgave him – never. I still haven't forgiven him. Years later, when he was sick and dying, I looked after him but I still could not forgive him. I have tried to forgive him since, but I just can't and that is something I have to live with.

The pain of those months was almost unbearable. I had no

friends. I didn't really fit in with the community on the site but after a while I knew I had to pull myself together. The survival instinct is very strong. I had to work to get money to find somewhere to live in order to get the boys back. Little did I know that from then on I would see them only during the school holidays, and it wouldn't be until they had grown up and left school that they would live with me again.

I took a job in a lampshade factory in Plumstead and worked there all the hours I could, taking as much overtime as they would give me. After about 18 months, I became friends with a lovely man called Ben who lived nearby. It was not a great romance. We just got friendly. He was older than me and single and I think we were both hungry for some kind of affection.

He owned a big caravan yard and most of his family lived there. He was a good man and easy to be with after all I had been through. Gradually, slowly, it turned into more than friendship and I moved in with him. When our beautiful daughter Gaynor was born I was 32 and we were both over the moon.

My gift hadn't disappeared. I was still 'seeing' things but I accepted that as part of everyday life. I had discovered that I had the gift of healing too. When I was a child in Eynsford I found that if I held a sick animal in my hands it would usually recover and when I was living with the boys in the caravan I discovered that, by putting my hands on people, I could cure them of their aches and pains. Now various people used to come asking me to heal their bad back or stiff shoulder and I would do my best. But on the whole we lived as any ordinary family.

All my life I have tried to explain to people that I am an ordinary woman. I know I have a gift, an extraordinary gift, but I am still an ordinary human being. Being psychic doesn't make you better or worse than anyone else and my everyday life is as ordinary as most people's.

Ben and I, and Gaynor, lived happily for years but in the end I fell out with his family who lived in the same yard, or they fell out with me and, sadly, Ben and I split up. It was time to move on. Once again I was alone with a child to bring up.

First, we went down to the country, fruit picking – just as Mum and Dad had done all those years ago. Then I did all sorts of jobs. When I was with Ben we worked at clearing houses of old furniture, so I still did a bit of that. Then I went to work in a biscuit factory. It wasn't exciting but it was an honest living.

Gaynor and I were living in a council flat in South London when one day I woke up with a start. I sat bolt upright in bed. Today my life was going to change. I did not know how – I just knew it would. I trusted that feeling completely, I always have, and I went out of the door knowing that things would be very different by the time I came back.

I was walking along the road when I saw a row of brand new houses. They were big and smart and once again my feet took me towards them as if they had a mind of their own. I knew I had to go onto the site and ask for a job. I was not even sure what that job was to be until I spoke to the workmen and found myself asking them who was doing the cleaning work in the houses. They told me an old man was getting £6 a house, but that he had recently left.

I went and saw the man in charge and said, 'I want the contract to clean these houses please.'

'How much?' he asked.

'Six pounds a house,' I said.

'Have you got your own crew?'

That, I have to admit, threw me.

'Oh yes, of course,' I said with phony confidence.

'Well, what's the name of your company, then?'

I thought fast, 'Saunders Cleaning Service.'

'How soon can you start?'

'This afternoon?'

'Done.'

And that, I discovered, is how big businesses are born!

There was no crew, of course, just me, and I rushed back home and got buckets and mops and scrubbing brushes and raided my cleaning cupboard for soap and disinfectant. Then I got back to the site and started scrubbing.

I knew how to scrub – I had done enough of that before – but running my own company was a complete mystery. The boss wanted to see my form P15 – what on earth was that? Then I had to find an accountant. I chose one from the phone book and told him what I was doing. He asked how much I had in the bank and when I told him £4, he took all my papers, tore them up and threw them in the bin. So I thought, 'Damn the lot of you, I'll do it myself.' And I did.

I remember when I got my first cheque for Saunders Cleaning Service and I thought, 'Shall I frame this or shall I put it in the bank?' Unfortunately, finances being as they were, I didn't really have the choice!

I got some leaflets printed about this wonderful 'company' and soon more work was piling in, so I started to hire other women. I was working 14 hours a day, seven days a week and I worked myself into the ground. The trouble with the job was that you had to get all the paint off the wooden floors and all the places the men had accidentally splashed. I would come home at night with my fingers bleeding and my knees scratched and sore like a small child who had fallen off her bicycle!

I didn't stop. It was almost as if I was possessed. I just wanted to prove that I could do it, that I could make something of myself. I still don't know who I wanted to impress – myself, most probably.

I do not know what I ended up proving, if anything, but I started with £4 and, in the second year of business, we turned over £14,000 and were working for all the big building firms like Bovis and Wimpey. All in all, I did jolly well.

For some reason, I did not 'see' as much as usual during these years. Of course, wherever I was working, it somehow got around that I had a gift and a lot of the workmen on whatever site I was working would come to me for healing when they strained their wrists or dropped a load of bricks on their foot. And, as usual, there were always times when I would look at a woman and think, 'Ooh, she's going to have a baby next year,' and 'Oh dear, he's going to be ill soon.'

But, mostly, I tried to ignore the gift as much as possible. I had fantasies about the business getting bigger and bigger. I was going to be a tycoon! Realistically, there was no way I could carry on the way I was going. Physically, I couldn't cope with it. I was working so hard, there was so much stress and tension and I paid little or no attention to my own well being. In return, my health started to fail me and I began to feel ill. By now I had fallen in love with a house in Bexleyheath. It was a wreck, a complete and utter wreck, but I was sure I could do something with it. So when the surveyor reported that, although it was a mess inside, it was structurally sound, I took out the £5,000 I had saved in the bank and put it down as a deposit. And I was in – my own house! I was thrilled to bits!

I had known as soon as I walked into the house that it was right for me. Yes, it is haunted. Most houses are. But the spirits welcomed me and I knew I would be happy within those walls and, as usual, my feelings were right. I have lived here ever since.

The house meant I had a big mortgage around my neck, so I carried on working, working, working. It was madness, really. Gradually, I felt worse and worse until I reached the stage where I could not get out of the bed and cross from one side of the room to the other.

The doctors thought I had leukaemia and, for the first time in my life I felt really ill, truly ill. Uncle Jack, an old family friend, had come to work for me and he lived at home as a lodger with Gaynor and me. He tried to carry on the business for me but he couldn't manage it.

One night I lay there in my front bedroom, feeling like death, and worrying about the desperate financial situation we were in. The doctors had told me I could not go back to work and I knew they were right, but it filled me with panic.

I thought, 'My God, what am I going to do?'

And He heard me and He gave me the answer. I heard a voice tell me that what I had to do was what I had been doing all along – giving clairvoyance. 'Make your living out of that,' He said. I had been so desperate for Him to tell me what to do, but once He had, it all seemed so obvious.

I trust God completely. I always have, and I had heard His voice before when I had let my faith slip a little. I remember once, when we were in the flat, I lay in bed and suddenly the rain was beating against the window and there were howling gales, apparently from nowhere. I've always been petrified of storms. Any drastic behaviour of the weather really frightens me because that's God's power, not mine, and as I lay there terrified, I heard a voice by the bed saying, 'Nella, where's your faith now?'

Immediately, I was overwhelmed with shame and within five minutes everything was at peace again. The storm died down so amazingly quickly that I spoke to the nextdoor neighbour about it the following morning. I said, 'Wasn't that storm amazing last night the way it suddenly stopped?'

She said, 'The storm raged all night.'

'No,' I said, 'it suddenly stopped blowing at eleven thirty.'

She gave me a funny look. 'Well, all I can say Nella is you must be a sound sleeper. The rest of us were kept awake all night.'

I should have trusted Him more after that. I should have had faith but, sometimes, we are so busy working, striving, thinking about the material things in life, that faith and the truth of life blurs and fades away for a while.

Now that I had heard the voice, I realised that, of course, He was right. I had been giving clairvoyance for years without even thinking about it.

It had always been there, of course. When I was healing people, spirits would sometimes come to me and tell me things. When I was healing a man who had lost his wife, suddenly I would hear her whisper to me, 'Tell him not to be so daft about our girl Mary – he's got to accept she's grown up now.'

Sometimes I would be chatting away and I would say without thinking, 'Oh well, you're planning this or that aren't you? So you've got that to look forward to.' I was giving clairvoyance while I healed people and, to me, it was a totally natural thing to do.

I have never charged for healing, and I never will, but the voice said I could charge for clairvoyance and that is just what I started to do. That message from beyond marked the end of my life as a charlady and the beginning of my career as a professional clairvoyant. I was 42 years old and, looking back, I can see now the pattern of my early life.

I now believe that everything I had gone through before, all the loving experiences, the sorrows, the joys and certainly the heartaches, were just to prepare me for the most important years of my life.

Everything that had gone before was training but when I reached my forties, only then was I mature enough to take on my life's work. Of course, there are times I look back on my earlier life with sadness and there are things I wish had never happened, like losing the boys when they were small. But there is a purpose to everything, you learn from every experience.

Even being so ill served a purpose. If I had not been ill I would not have stopped work, which means I would still have been running the cleaning business and I would not have begun my career as a clairvoyant.

I have no regrets – except one. I wish when I was a child I had not been made to feel so different because of my gift. I wish a grown-up had told me that it *was* a gift, something I could treasure, something totally natural, instead of always feeling that, because of it, I didn't 'belong'. I wish I had never had the 'lonely feeling' that no one could understand, or even wanted to understand, the strange experiences I had and the strange things I saw.

I believe every child is psychic. I believe all of us are psychic. In some of us the gift is stronger but we all have the power and often the gift is greatest when we are children, even though we can't, at that age, understand or control it.

I believe that many children see spirits from the other side. I would go further than that, I think almost all children see spirits from the other side at some time or another.

Children can see them so easily because their minds haven't been cluttered up with everything else – all the luggage we carry from the material world. From the age children start to run about and talk they are conditioned into this modern way of life, into what they should do and what they should not do; what they should be like and what they should not be like.

Then, we cram them full of learning. We say, 'This is a picture of this and that is a picture of that,' and we say, 'Repeat after me . . .' and their poor little minds become full of our indoctrination.

We do not place nearly enough emphasis on the spiritual side of life to our children. Nothing should be rigid. Yes, of course, there must be discipline, of course rules have to be made, standards have to be set down which we, and they, must try and live by, and of course there must be education.

But the mind has got to be free. If this world is going to progress at all, our minds have to be free. The worst thing you can say to a psychic child – any child – is, 'Don't be silly,' just because they can see or sense things that you can't. For then the child thinks, 'I must block these psychic feelings off', and the poor things do block them off, otherwise they know they will get into trouble, just like I did. I tried to block off those feelings, too, but mine didn't go away.

I believe children are conscious of these psychic feelings when they are very, very young. Even before a child can talk, you might find him lying in his cot and, suddenly, he will look in a certain direction in the room and his attention is held, although there seems to be nothing there. He will probably smile, gurgle and he will look as if he is listening and watching something.

That child has seen a spirit.

Then, when children begin to talk you will find that, occasionally, they will come out with something that they could not possibly know and you will think, 'Where on earth did they learn that?' Then, most probably you will dismiss it. But you shouldn't.

I have seen it with my own grandchildren. When my little grandson James was only 15 months old we took him for a walk in the fields and he pointed to something deep in the grass and said, 'That's a thistle.'

How did that child know it was a thistle? No one had ever talked about thistles or shown him pictures of thistles. We kept on, 'What is that darling?'

He looked at us as if we were daft and he kept saying, 'It's a this-tle.' He just knew it.

There are other teachers besides those in our earthly schools. There are teachers, I am sure, from the other side as well as this side.

Three to five years is, I think, the most psychic age for little ones. Then they go to school and start losing it. By the time they are eight it is often gone, buried deep inside them, smothered by everything else, imprisoned in the subconscious.

But, before that, most children can see spirits easily. They meet imaginary friends that they talk to and their parents say, 'Don't be silly.' But how do parents know that the child hasn't got a little spirit child with them? I believe they have.

Sometimes spirit children come back just to play with other chil-dren, like the children who used to come and see me at Home Farm.

It is lovely. I was not frightened. It was beautiful and I loved our friendship. I loved every minute of it.

Sometimes, children come back just for fun but sometimes, if the child has met with a violent death, he or she doesn't immediately realise he is dead so the little spirit remains earthbound for a time. And, because children are so sensitive and so in tune with the other dimension, it is only natural that the spirit children feel an empathy with them and believe they are people they can make contact with.

With some spirit children it takes a long time for them to come to terms with the fact that they are dead but, eventually, they do and they meet other lovely spirits, older souls, who help them with that realisa-tion; spirits who guide them and say, 'Look – this is your world now – you have left that earthly world.'

If a child is lonely, of course, he may invent an imaginary friend. But that is not the whole story, I am quite convinced of it.

I don't think there are any hard and fast rules you can apply. Naturally, people like to think that if a child dies it stays with its par-ents in spirit – if the parents have any belief in the spirit world. But that is not necessarily true. A child's spirit goes where it wants to go, it is a free little spirit.

Sometimes, I believe a child is sent back to earth as another child. There has been a lot of research in this country, and all over the world, into reincarnation. The case that sticks in my mind is of a little English boy who was being taken somewhere for the first time and sud-denly he pointed to a house and said, 'I used to live there.'

Thank God, his parents were not sceptical about it. They just said, 'You used to live there?'

Then the boy said, 'Oh yes, I was killed when I lived there,' and he went on to list what his name had been, how he was seven when he died, the names of his other mother, father, brother and sister.

What these sensible people did then was to go back to the area and research what the boy had said, and they found that everything their son had told them was correct. A child by that name had lived at that address. His mother, father, brother and sister were named as he had said and he had been killed when he was seven. I am sure he is not alone. Many children have a memory of their former life.

Sometimes children who die stay for a long while as spirit children; others grow up in spirit. Some poltergeists are just mischievous young spirits who want to have fun and games. Often, a poltergeist is the spirit of a fourteen or fifteen-year-old merely having a bit of a laugh and they probably cannot understand why the earthbound people in the house they are haunting cannot share the joke.

There are no firm rules, but I believe the psychic power of a child goes in seven-year cycles. A child, up to the age of seven, may take it for granted that he sees spirits or that funny things happen. After seven he blocks it out. But about seven years later, when he's around fourteen and about to lose his childhood, then he is very likely to be visited by spirits.

At that stage he has neither the mind of a child nor the mind of an adult. He is rebellious and his mind is open to the world, so spirits of the same age, who are also at their most mischievous, sense that they will be welcome to visit him. Teenage children are easy targets.

So if your child says, 'I've got this friend who comes to see me at night,' don't panic. Try and accept it as perfectly normal. And you can easily find out if it is an imaginary child or a spirit child.

All you have to do is ask questions about the friend, 'Where does your friend come from? What's her name? How old is she? Did she ever live in this house? When did she live in this house?'

With an imaginary child friend your child will probably stumble over the answers. He does not know the answers because he has not imagined them yet. But the child with a spirit friend will reply to the questions quickly and easily because the spirit child is there behind him, telling him all he needs to know. You can either encourage the friendship or discourage it. But, I think that if a child wants to talk about their secret or special friend, let them talk about it. That is healthy.

If a child starts to tell you of things that are going to happen, but haven't happened yet, don't mock them. For God's sake, listen.

I wish someone had said to me, 'Well, this is a gift – don't worry about it. This is a gift, use it properly, use it to benefit mankind not destroy it, because if you use it for destructive purposes you only destroy yourself.' All children must learn that.

Being psychic is natural. There is nothing spooky about it. There is nothing unusual about it. It is the most natural thing in the world. If people could treat it as normal, youngsters would learn to accept it as such.

Try not to smother the gifts of your psychic child with ridicule or scepticism because, once buried, it is so difficult to bring it back to the surface when you are an adult. It is the sheer innocence of childhood that is so beautiful

And innocence, that ability to look with wonder at the world and realise we don't understand even half of it, is really the key to our psychic selves.

TWO

The Psychic Detective

'Obviously any information, from any source, is always listened to and we are grateful to hear from anybody who thinks they can help the police. But it is not the policy of the Metropolitan police to actively seek help from clairvoyants.'

SPOKESWOMAN, NEW SCOTLAND YARD
MARCH 1992

'A young woman was found dead in a local park in early February, 1991, but, after eight months of hard work, our murder inquiry was, frankly, getting nowhere. A colleague and I consulted a senior officer and we then decided to call on Nella for help.

'I had never met Nella before, although I had heard of her reputation from fellow officers who said she had come up with some very useful leads on other cases in the past.

'We took Nella to the park and we asked her if she wanted us to show her where the murder had been committed. She said no and then proceeded to take us to the exact spot where the girl had been killed. It was quite extraordinary.

'She said, "This is where a struggle took place, and this is where he dropped a piece of paper on the ground. And this is where he jumped over the railings and then ran away."

'She was right on all counts. We had found a piece of paper at that spot, which we believed may have belonged to the murderer, and, where Nella said he had jumped over the railings, we had found forensic evidence which suggested just that.

'You could call that coincidence or plain good luck, but the railings ran for 200 feet and she was spot on.

'She told us details of the case which only the police knew. These facts had not been made public so there's no way she could have read about them in the newspapers.

'Her description of the girl, her personality, and the kind of life she had lived, were uncannily accurate. She gave us several new leads which we followed up. In the end, we did not get our man and the case is still open, but I don't think you can blame Nella for that because we came to her very late in the day – eight months after the crime had been committed. Also, in this country, police officers are not used to working with mediums, so perhaps we don't know how to pose the questions in the right way to get the most useful answers.

'Personally, I believe psychics do have a valuable role to play in police work. I have worked with several mediums like Nella and they have all been very useful.

'I would like to see them used far more often by the police when we find ourselves up against a brick wall. This often happens in the United States but, here, many officers are loath to call in psychics. They fear ridicule and the public think that "The Great Detective" should be able to solve the case all on his own, like some character from fiction! That's nonsense. There's also the attitude, "Why pay detectives at all if you can get psychics to do all the work?" That's plain silly.

'I don't know how Nella does it. I don't think she understands fully herself. But no one can deny that she has an extraordinary talent.'

DETECTIVE CONSTABLE NEIL PRATT,
SOUTH LONDON POLICE
1992

'Seven years ago I bumped into Nella at Belvedere police station and almost the first thing she told me was that the following day I would be going to Gravesend to arrest a man I had been searching for. She told me I would be going to a caravan site, she even told me the colour of the caravan I would visit and some other details. I was totally amazed. These were things I'd only just found out myself. There was no way she could have known.

'Since then Nella has helped me on several cases and always her information has been very valuable and amazingly accurate. Once, I took her to a house where an old lady had been robbed and attacked and she described to me exactly what had happened: how the old lady had been pushed against the wall, how she had fallen in the kitchen hitting her head on an old spin dryer as she went down. We knew that but Nella could not possibly have known.

'I had never been a great believer in psychic power but the details she was giving me made my hair stand up on end.

'Sometimes she knows about the cases I work on even before I do!

'She once asked me how I was getting on with the case of the murder of a young girl who had been battered to death and whose body had been dumped many miles from the scene of the crime. I was working on no such case and told her so.

'The next day I went into the station and there was the report on my desk of a murder case – a young girl battered to death – that had been resurrected after seven years. All the details were exactly as Nella described.

'I can't explain how Nella knows these things. It defies all logical explanation and, as a policeman, everything I work on has to have a logical basis. I am naturally sceptical, but almost everything Nella has told me has been a hundred per cent true, so I am baffled.

'Of course, the police force, as an organisation, are worried that they would be ridiculed if it were known that they called in psychics. Few psychics have the track record that Nella has and if the police opened up and said "Yes, we will use psychics," you could get a lot of cranks on the doorstep.

'I don't think it should be a matter of force policy: it must be up to individual officers. I have never approached Nella to help with a case – she has always come to me – but I know other officers who have, and I know that all the officers who have dealt with Nella on various cases would go back to her for help again.

'No, she is not right all the time but she's more often right than wrong. Certainly, if I were working on a murder case now, and I was getting nowhere, I would go to her. What would I have to lose?

'We, the police, are an investigative body and whatever information we get we have to act upon, unless of course it's obviously from a crank.

'Given Nella's track record, bearing in mind how she has helped me and other police officers I know in criminal cases, I would say that any policeman who dismissed, out of hand, the information Nella gave to him would be making a very unwise move.

'She is the one detective who never gives evidence in court but she is a good detective nonetheless.'

DETECTIVE INSPECTOR DON MIDDLETON, METROPOLITAN
POLICE
MARCH 1992

Pain. Terrible pain. Please stop hurting me. Please don't. I'm frightened. I feel sick. Why does he have to crush my fingers? Why do you have to crush my fingers? Somebody help me . . .

I was lying on the floor and he was beating me. Except I was not lying on the floor and the two burly policemen I was with were merely watching me. But that is how it felt and those are the thoughts that were rushing through my mind.

The murder last year of a lady I'll call Mrs Box was one of the worst cases I have ever worked on. She was 75 years old and happily married. She was a mother and a grandmother, and she was bludgeoned to death.

I have been working with the police for nearly 20 years now. You never get immune to the suffering but, for some reason, this case affected me more than any other since the Yorkshire Ripper murders of the early 1980s. As this case is still going through the legal system I have had to change the names and some of the details, but I would like to tell you this story. It shows you how I work but, also, I think the horror of what happened to Mrs Box, in Britain in the 1990s, is a story that should be told.

For me the case started, like most of them do, with a phone call.

'Hello Nella, we're police inspectors. We know you've done a lot of work for a colleague of ours in the past so we wondered if you could help us out with this case.'

'Well,' I said, 'I'll do my best.'

They did not tell me what case it was and I did not ask. I avoid watching crime stories on the television news most of the time because they affect me so badly. Horrific pictures flash into my mind and I can feel the pain. If I watch them every day it really does get too much for me to cope with.

So, when the policeman came and asked me if I had heard about the murder of this woman I said, in all honesty, no. It rang a very vague bell but nothing more.

We were sitting at my dining room table and I had a piece of paper beside me. As they told me, briefly, about a woman being murdered, I found myself drawing shapes all over the paper.

'I don't know why I'm drawing these shapes,' I said, 'but it must mean something. Does it mean anything?'

One of the coppers went white.

'It's her name,' he said. 'These shapes – that's the name of the murdered woman.'

The police had not brought anything for me to look at, or to hold, but suddenly I could see a building in my mind.

I did not know where it was, I had certainly never been there, but I described the interior of it with confidence. I said, 'There's this piece of furniture here and a table on your left and then you go down some stairs and there's another room full of furniture down there.' I described the whole layout.

27

Then I asked, 'Who's Y? Who's Y?'

'I don't believe I'm hearing all this,' said one of the officers. I ignored him. I was in full flow by then.

I said, 'Well, somehow he's involved with Mrs Box.'

'Y is someone who's done work for Mrs Box in the past,' they said.

'Don't look towards him. He's not involved in the murder. But maybe he does know more than he thinks he knows. There are some things he knows which are more important than he realises. You should question him further.'

Then I heard a name very strongly.

'Mr X. Who's Mr X?' I asked them. 'You've dismissed Mr X. Don't dismiss Mr X. You must have a closer look at Mr X.'

And that was all I got.

The policemen did not say much as they left, they rarely do, and I put the whole episode out of my mind, although I had a feeling that this was not the end of the story. And two days later they rang back. Could they come and see me again?

They turned up in an unmarked police car and then they said they didn't want me just to talk to them, they wanted to take me to the scene of the crime. Before we left I drew a man's face on a piece of paper, a face that kept coming to me.

We drove to the building in a fashionable street. As soon as I got out of the car the strangest feeling came over me. I wasn't Nella any more, I was a man, a homosexual man. I was walking up and down outside the building in a very camp way. I felt I *was* this man and next I was talking as he did and all my mannerisms, the way I moved, were his.

I could see him as clear as day. I said, 'This is him, this is the man in my picture. This is what he looks like. And he's got a mark on his ear, here.'

One of the policemen was startled. 'I know who you're talking about, I know who you mean.'

'Well,' I said, 'Why have you dismissed this man?'

'He's OK,' said the police officer. 'We've checked him out but he's OK.'

'No, he's not,' I said.

As we went into the building I felt the man leaving me. I was Nella again. Then, suddenly, I wasn't Nella. I was Mrs Box. I felt I was her. The building was just as I had described it to the police on their first visit, although I was surprised it was so sparse. When I had seen it at home it was choc-a-bloc. Now it was almost empty. A chair or two here and there and a polished wooden desk in the corner but, apart from that, virtually nothing. Perhaps the police, or the lady's family, had moved most of the furniture out.

Standing there I could hear myself talking, but they were not my words, the words came from Mrs Box.

She was in the building. She was looking at her murderer and she was saying, 'What would Peter think if he knew you were doing this? What would Peter think?'

One of the detectives nearly fell over.

'What did you say, Nella?'

'You should be listening to everything I say and writing it down,' I said firmly. 'Do you know who Peter is?'

'Yes,' he said. 'He's a close friend of Mr X.'

Then I heard the murderer order Mrs Cross downstairs to the lower part of the building I was talking to him. I mean, Mrs Box was talking to him, as we went down the stairs. He was behind me – behind her.

Near the bottom of the stairs he must have hit her from behind because when I got there I was reeling, I felt I was falling and I had to grab hold of the bannister. I felt terribly sick.

I managed to get into the room. Then I looked at the floor. It was bare.

'No,' I said, 'It wasn't like this. No, when I was lying here on the floor I was lying on a light-coloured carpet.' I sat down at an old desk.

'This has been changed too. It wasn't like this. This has been moved. I think at some point he sat here – later. Now I am falling onto my hands and knees. He is beating me. I am in pain. Pain. He is hurting my arm.

'There's someone at the door. I can hear someone at the door trying to get in. They're trying the door but it's locked. They haven't got their key. They're going away.

'I want to be sick. I feel sick. He is hurting me. He's taken a necklace from around my neck. He's just snatched it away from me. Why is he doing this?'

I described the necklace.

I felt terrible. I knew that my fingers had been crushed and that my arm was nearly broken, it was black and blue. While I was down in that room I felt really ill but, as we walked back up the stairs, I began to feel better and I knew we had to go somewhere else.

'Follow me,' I said to the police officers. We went out of the building, turned right and right again. I pointed to a restaurant. 'She used to sit in that restaurant,' I said. 'But they don't know anything. You won't get any information there.'

Then I stopped. 'And this is where Mr X parked his car,' I said.

'Mr X doesn't drive,' they said.

'Yes, he does and I can show you what sort of car it is.' We walked up the road until we came to a small blue car. 'This isn't his car but his car is exactly like this. It's the same colour and the same make.'

By now, I felt totally drained and the police said they would take me home, and we drove in silence, each lost in our own thoughts of the terrible crime. 'There is something I have missed,' I thought, as we headed over the river. 'There is something else, something niggling at me.'

29

'He left something in the building,' I said suddenly. 'He doesn't realise it, but he left something behind. Something small.'

Then I felt I was Mrs Box again. I kept holding my right ear. I said 'Oh my God, where's my other earring?'

The policeman stopped the car.

'What are you saying Nella?'

I said, 'My earring is missing. He ripped it out of my ear so my ear was split. Why did he do that to me? Why did he crush my fingers?'

The policemen were stunned and we continued our journey in silence.

I felt the poor woman was with me all the way home. I honestly think she came back to me to explain what had happened because she wanted her murderer caught. When they left me at home I felt unwell but I made myself a cup of tea and put on some music and tried to relax. She left me then but I felt unwell for several days afterwards.

The case would not go away. I had told the police that I kept thinking about Dover in connection with Mr X, and there was something about a dealer but it was all very mixed up and confused. And the idea of the floor, that bare floor, kept worrying me.

Some time later they rang me again. Unfortunately I don't get much feedback from the police. They pick my brains but they hold their own counsel and they rarely tell me if I was right or wrong. But this time the Inspector was kind enough to call me.

'You were right about Mrs Box,' he said, and he told me I had described her injuries correctly including her split ear and poor crushed fingers. Mr X did drive a blue car, just as I had described, and they had found something small the murderer had accidentally left behind in the building. And Mr X was also involved in business in Dover.

'And what about the floor? The floor was wrong.'

'Yes,' he said. 'There was a cream-coloured carpet on the floor but we took it away to forensics.'

Not long afterwards Mr X was arrested and charged with murder. The case has yet to be heard and I await, with interest, to see how right or wrong I was.

I have not forgotten Mrs Box or the time she spent 'with me'. There was a good feeling about that woman and her death was a tragedy. I felt I knew her – albeit briefly. She was a gentle person, yet she was a strong character. She was dignied and very charming, very self-possessed. I hope for her familys sake, and for her sake, that justice will be done and she can rest in peace.

I have been working for the police on and off for nearly twenty years. It all started in 1974 when a seventeenth-century painting by Vermeer, called *The Guitar Player* and worth £2,000,000, was stolen from a beautiful place called Kenwood House on London's Hampstead Heath.

Before then I might see a story about a crime in the newspaper, or hear details mentioned on the television, and I would think, 'I know who did that' or 'idiot police – they're all looking in the wrong place for him.' But then I would tell myself to shut up. 'It's nothing to do with you Nella,' I used to think. And, anyway, I didn't want to get involved. By that time I was working my insides out with the cleaning business so I didn't have much time for anything else.

But, somehow, this crime was different. It was Sunday evening and I was watching the television out of half an eye while I waded through a pile of ironing. I was really only half listening when they flashed a picture of a big white house up onto the screen and they were talking about this fantastic art robbery. Almost without thinking, I said 'Well, of course they haven't found them, they're looking in the wrong place.'

Then pictures started coming into my mind which I just could not push away. I ran into Gaynor's room and grabbed a piece of her drawing paper and a pencil.

I often get the urge to draw things when I am working on a crime and this time, without thinking, I drew a map and, on it, two crosses. Then I kept saying to myself, 'Come on Nella – more'.

I have never been to Kenwood House in my life but I drew the back of the building, not the front: a big open field, trees and a mesh fence. I could see it all in my mind and I knew exactly where the police had to go to find something important to do with the case.

I sat looking at my piece of paper and thinking, 'Well, now what?' I had never phoned the police in my life before but I thought 'I've got to do something about this. I am right. I know I am right'. So I thought, 'To hell with it,' and I picked up the phone and rang Scotland Yard.

I didn't tell them who I was, I just said I had some information about the robbery which might interest them and they told me to ring the police at Hampstead, which I did.

'I've got some information about the Kenwood House robbery,' I said.

'Who are you madam?'

'Well, I'm a clairvoyant actually,' I said. After all, it is the truth and I can't get away from that. I never feel embarrassed about telling the truth.

'I see, madam. What do you want to tell us madam?'

So I told him all that I had seen in my vision. I said, 'If you stand behind Kenwood House with your back to the house and look straight ahead, as if that is 12 o'clock, at 11 o'clock there's a kind of lane and if you go down this lane there's a little pond and some railings and over there you'll find something to do with the picture.'

I thought he might say, 'We'll be right round with the little green van to whisk you off to the loony bin,' but he made no comment – just, 'Thank you very much madam, we'll pass this on madam.'

And that was that. 'Well,' I thought, 'I've told them. I've done my duty. Now it's up to them.'

Five minutes later the phone rang. 'Oh hello madam, it's Hampstead CID here. Do you think you could along and help us?'

So, being naive of course, what else could I say but yes.

They came and picked me up and took me to the police station. This first time I was not allowed up into the incident room where the real work goes on. Instead, they kept me in a little room downstairs and two policemen came to talk to me, Detective Constable Jim Bayes and Detective Constable Dave Morgan.

From the start I could sense this Jim Bayes did not like me. He was very anti-me and I did not like him much either. But the other one, Dave, I liked from the start and I thought, 'I can work well with him'. It was a bit like Maggie Thatcher saying about President Gorbachev when they met, 'Yes, I can do business with him.'

'Where do you want to go, Nella?' Dave asked.

'Hampstead. To the big house. Here's my map,' I said, and gave him my scrap of drawing paper.

He looked surprised but did not say much except, 'Have you been to Kenwood House before?'

'No,' I said in all honesty. 'I didn't even know it existed until I saw it on the television. I've never even been to Hampstead.'

As we drove there I was talking about a mesh fence at the back of the house and Jim Bayes seemed to take great delight in telling me that there was no such fence there.

'Yes, there is,' I said. 'A diamond mesh fence.' And, when we arrived, there it was – a brand new diamond mesh fence. I have to admit that the look on Jim Bayes' face gave me a great deal of pleasure!

We climbed over the fence and started walking. I will never forget how cold it was. Snow was falling lightly and I felt chilled literally to my bones. But I walked on. I knew where I was going. At least, I didn't know where I was going, but I knew enough about my gift to know that I had to trust my instincts. As long as I trust my feelings, my feet will inevitably lead me in the right direction.

'What are we looking for?' asked Jim Bayes; cold, fed up and quite obviously convinced that this was all a waste of time.

'I don't know,' I said. 'But it's metal and it's very important.'

As we approached the lake I had a strong feeling that we had arrived at the right place.

'Stay close,' I told them. 'Stay close to me because we're almost on it.'

I stopped dead. There at my feet lay pieces from the alarm box from the back of the painting. What I felt then is so hard to describe. It's a sensation that starts in my stomach and gets stronger, until I am all knotted up inside. I thought, 'This is it. I knew it was here. I've done it. I was right.'

The police had missed the alarm box, even the sniffer dogs they had brought in had missed it, but I had taken them straight to it. The two policemen were non-plussed. They did not quite know what to do. They were not sure whether to run me in, to leave me standing there while they took the alarm over to the other detectives who were waiting across the field, or what. So Dave Morgan stayed with me while, very gingerly using a handkerchief so he wouldn't ruin any fingerprints, Jim Bayes picked up the alarm and took it to their senior officers.

It was only as we were driving back to Hampstead police station that Dave Morgan told me that they had found the picture's frame exactly where I had told them to look earlier – down the lane, past the pond and over the railings.

We got back to the police station and this time they walked me straight past the little room. Instead, I was taken up to the incident room to meet the big white chief, Chief Superintendent Arthur Pike, who was in charge of the case.

'Well done, Nella,' he said. 'When did you put it there?'

I looked at him. 'Typical policeman,' I said. 'Suspicious!'

He smiled. 'So where do you want to go now?'

I said 'I can see big black gates and caves.'

'Caves,' he said. 'Go on.'

I described what I could see: caves under the ground, overgrown shrubbery, quiet, dark.

'That sounds like Highgate Cemetery. The part that's not used,' he said. I took his word for it and Dave, Jim and I set off for Highgate.

In the car I gave Jim a drawing I had done of a man's face. It had come to me while I was sitting at home. I did not know who he was, but I knew it was a psychic clue and that I had to show this picture to someone.

I said to Jim and Dave, 'Right now, there is someone there watching the painting. When we get to the gate there's a tiny gate-keeper's hut on the right where a man sits. Will you show him my drawing?'

Jim Bayes was impatient. 'No, we'll do that later. Come on, not now.'

We went on into the cemetery and walked up a path. There was high ground and graves in front of us and suddenly Dave Morgan leaned over to me. 'Keep your voice down love,' he said. 'We're being watched.' I looked up but I could see nothing.

Dave went one way and Jim the other and I was left standing on the path all by myself and I thought, 'What the hell am I doing here?' It was really spooky – and I am not spooked easily. I was frightened the man, whoever he was, would double back and come after me. So, I stood there, rooted to the spot, and prayed for the policemen to come back. They did a short while later, empty-handed. The man had got away.

We walked on up the path and then there they were, the cata-combs, just as I had described. It was a terrible sight. The graves had been ransacked and the bodies desecrated. There were skulls and bones everywhere.

'The painting has been hidden in one of these catacombs,' I said. 'And if it's not out of here by Sunday it will be taken away and hidden in another cemetery.'

But Jim and Dave were not prepared to go in there and search all the caves. To be honest, I can't say I blamed them. All three of us could not wait to get away from that place. To me, there is nothing creepy about a corpse. Once a person dies their spirit leaves their body and all that is left is skin and bones. But there was an atmosphere I did not like at that place, something very unpleasant. We went back down the path to the gatekeeper's hut. I said, 'I'm not leaving until you show that man my drawing.'

Jim shrugged and took it out of his pocket and showed it to the little man who was watching us.

'Oh blimey, not him again,' he said.

'You know him?'

'So do you. You've already got him in nick for desecrating all these graves.'

When we got back to the police station I saw Arthur Pike again and showed him the drawing.

He told me no picture of this man had ever been published. There was no way I could have seen that man's face before. But Chief Inspector Pike did have a mug shot of him taken when the man had been arrested.

'Show me your drawing, Nella,' he said and he put my drawing beside the mug shot. They were almost identical. But that did not help us with the painting. I had merely picked up his face because of what he had done in the catacombs.

Again I told them that they ought to search there thoroughly but they fobbed me off. 'Leave it with us,' they said. If I have heard that once I have heard it a thousand times from policemen working on dozens of crimes. 'Leave it with us.'

Well, I thought, I had done my best and it had been a long day. No lunch, just one cup of tea, and I was exhausted.

From that day on I kept in touch with the police by phone. I predicted the arrival of every ransom letter from the thieves and I predicted that the police would get one ransom note together with an actual piece of the painting. I even told them which corner of the painting it would come from.

I did my best to help them but something very strange started to happen. After a few days I was sure I was being watched. It made me feel quite ill, until I realised that it was the police who were having me tailed. They even had my phone tapped, which annoyed me intensely, but I tried to ignore it. I had obviously done something right otherwise they would not have bothered and, when I wasn't feeling angry about it, I was amused that the police actually thought I might be involved in the theft.

The case dragged on and it would not leave me alone. Life would continue as usual and then, suddenly, something would flash into my mind: a date, a picture of another letter.

One day, I knew that the next thing the thieves were going to do was to threaten to burn the painting. I rang Illyd Harrington, the chairman of the Greater London Council which actually owned the picture, and told him not to worry.

'Don't worry, Mr Harrington. The picture won't be burned. It will be found in a cemetery just as I told you it would.'

Some time later *The Guitar Player* by Jan Vermeer was found in a cemetery next to St Bartholomew's Hospital in London. The police never thanked me for my help. I was not paid – I am never paid. They did not even pay my cleaning bills and, after tramping through the shrubbery at the back of Kenwood House, my best coat was absolutely ruined. At least they stopped having me followed and they stopped tapping my phone.

I thought the police had probably forgotten all about me, but no. Word got around and it was not long before other police officers came to call, asking if I could help out.

The lads from the local police station, the CID mob, began to make a habit of coming around to my house every Friday night. The doorbell would ring and there they would be on the doorstep.

'Oh hello, Nella,' one would say. 'We just happened to be round this way so we thought we'd drop in for a cup of tea.'

And I would think, 'You lying so and so, you've come to pick my brains again!'

We would sit around chatting by the fire and, usually, it was not long before I picked up something about a case and, then, I would tell them what they were working on. Nine times out of ten I was right and then they would say, 'Now, what about this case . . .'

One of my biggest problems when I am working on any crime is timing. What is time? Time is meaningless. I can see backwards in time and I can see forwards in time. Sometimes I see a specific date – it flashes up in front of my eyes – but, at other times, I can see a crime taking place but I can't fix it to a day or month.

One Friday, I was sitting there trying to help the lads out with a bank robbery they were working on, when I suddenly said, 'What happened about the double murder down in Brighton?'

They all looked baffled.

'What double murder?'

Then, I could see it all as if I was up on the ceiling looking down. One of the detectives, Chalky White they called him, grabbed a pen and started writing everything down in his diary.

'It's Brighton. There's an antique shop and it has a flat upstairs. In the flat there's a man and a woman in bed. She's out cold, blind drunk. He's drunk too, but he's still awake.

'A man's come in. He's wearing one earring. He's coming up the stairs, he's got a knife. There's an almighty scuffle. Murder, murder!

There's blood everywhere. He's killed them.

'He's going downstairs and out to the back of the shop. There's a can of paraffin there. He's picking it up and sprinkling paraffin around the shop. He's set it alight and now he's going out, he's running away. The whole shop is burning. The flames are going up, up, up.'

I could see it all with my eyes wide open and Chalky was writing it all down. Then the pictures faded. By now, the policemen knew me well enough to take me seriously and they didn't waste any time in getting onto their colleagues in the CID at Brighton.

They said 'Got any more on this double murder at the antique shop?'

But the detectives there said, 'What double murder? We haven't got a double murder. We don't know anything about an antique shop.'

The policemen questioned me again and again and I tried to pinpoint the exact address of the antique shop, but the pictures had faded and I couldn't get them back. The police even visited a few antique shops in Brighton, but they found nothing.

Two months later, almost two months to the day, a constable was patrolling in Brighton in the early hours of the morning when he spotted an antique shop on fire. When the firemen had doused the flames, and forced their way in, they found two bodies – a woman and a man, both dead. A knife was in the man's back and the woman had been battered to death. The man, the police later discovered, was a drug addict and the woman, his girlfriend, was an alcoholic.

I only heard all this when the police in Brighton rang me up. They wanted me to try and go back into my 'vision', as they called it, and try and find out where the man had gone.

The words came straight into my head.

I said, 'You'll find him in Lewes market.' Lewes is a town a few miles inland from Brighton.

Sure enough they did find him in Lewes market – twelve years later! It wasn't until 1990 that police arrested a man and charged him with the double murder. He is now in prison.

So, you see, time is tricky. I know what I see is true but when did it happen? Was it yesterday? Or is it tomorrow?

I am often asked what it feels like when I see a crime. There is no simple answer. With poor Mrs Box I feel the pain and I feel the fear. Of course, it upsets me, I may be psychic but I am only human. I always feel the horror of the murder and that terror is something that no one who has not experienced it can ever understand. Often, when I am working on a particularly horrible case, I can feel physically sick for days afterwards.

I do not belong to that school of thought which says that these people who commit violent crime are not bad, but mad – that they are somehow not responsible for their actions. I know that is true of some cases, but I also know that there are a lot of evil people in this world. I know it, I can feel their evil, and these people care little about the consequences of their actions.

All the crimes I work on upset me, but it is the ones when I can feel the fear and terror of the vulnerable, the very old and the very young, which are the worst. Violent crimes against elderly people make me sick to my soul.

I was involved in a shocking case a couple of years ago. There were two elderly sisters, in their late seventies or early eighties, and they lived together in a little terraced house in Peckham, South London.

One day someone broke into the house and beat one of the old ladies to death.

The police had been working on the case for months before they came to me. One day a detective turned up on the doorstep. He was totally honest about it. 'We're on this murder case, Nella, and we haven't got anywhere. We've come up against a brick wall. Can you help us? This is official.'

I remember him saying that – 'This is official.' It stuck in my mind because it was unusual for the police to admit they were asking for my help officially. I asked him to take me to the scene of the crime. Sometimes that is not necessary. I can work at home with maps, or photos, or often with nothing at all. I can just kind of tune in. But, in some cases, like this one, I actually feel drawn to the place where the tragedy happened.

It was a sad scene. The other old lady had been there apparently when her sister was murdered but, afterwards, she was in such a terrible state of shock she could not tell the police anything.

After the murder she never uttered a word, the poor old soul. The shock was too much for her. She, too, had been beaten and she was still so frightened that her relatives came and took her away. The house was dismal and cold, with an overwhelming atmosphere of sadness and emptiness. It was just a little house, there was nothing at all grand about it, but it was homely and the sisters had obviously kept it spick and span.

I stood in one place in the hall and told the detective: 'A scuffle took place here and there's definitely more than one person. I think three of them came into the house.'

I got the initial 'A' very strongly and then my feet took me upstairs to the back bedroom.

I said, 'They came in through this window and the old lady was beaten up terribly here.'

'She was murdered here,' he said.

'No,' I said. 'She didn't die in this room. She was taken into the front room, the front bedroom, by someone else and she died in there.'

I went downstairs and sat in the tiny lounge looking out of the window onto the road and casting my mind back to the night of the murder.

I said, 'There's an old red Ford Cortina out there with a roof rack that's all rusty.'

He jumped up to take a look.

'No, it's not there now, but it was there on the night of the murder.'

Suddenly a name came into my mind. Earl. E-A-R-L. I was spelling it out. I kept saying it over and over again. I did not know what it meant but I knew it was important.

'What do we do now?' he asked.

'I follow my nose.'

'OK,' he said. 'You follow your nose and we'll follow you.'

'I want to find a pet shop and I've got to get behind the pet shop and there's a big open space and a tin fence down the side.'

'Well, you go where you want to go and we'll follow, Nell.'

I went out of the house and I turned left. That took us to a main road and there, opposite me, was a pet shop. I was on the right track. I went into the pet shop and asked them if they employed anyone called Earl. They said no, and looked at me as if I was a bit daft, but that didn't bother me. It never does, I get those looks all the time.

So, we left the pet shop, I turned sharp left and there was the big open space I had seen in my mind and there was my tin fence. I thought, 'You're going the right way, Nell. Keep on.'

We got to the end of the fence and one of the officers turned to the inspector and said, 'Guv, look – Earl Road.'

'I'm not finished yet,' I said and they followed me on down the road until I came to a second-hand car garage.

The policemen looked at me expectantly.

'The case ends here,' I said. 'Go in and ask them questions. As far as I'm concerned the case is over.' I was exhausted. I am always exhausted at the end of a case and all I wanted to do was go home.

Weeks went by and I heard nothing. Then I answered the phone one day and it was the detective.

'It's only fair I should tell you Nella. Everything you said was spot on.'

It turned out that there were four young lads involved in the break-in and murder. On the night of the murder they were driving an old, battered, red Ford Cortina with a rusty roof rack and a week later they had sold it tothe second-hand garage. One of them was called Albert. Two of the culprits were arrested immediately. Two of them ran away to Ireland but I believe they were caught later.

Justice was done but the case made me despair. The motive was robbery. I do not know exactly what they took from the old ladies because the police never enlighten me with details like that, but, having looked around that little terraced house, what could there possibly have been there of great value?

Sometimes, when I am working on a crime, it is very difficult to tune into one case and that case alone. If the police officers involved have been working on another case at the same time, I sometimes pick up details of that one instead.

Sometimes spirits from the other side will come through to me and tell me about other murders they are worried about. It can all end up as such a jumble in my mind, it is hard to sort the wheat from the chaff. That happened to me frequently when I was working on the case of the Yorkshire Ripper, Peter Sutcliffe, the man jailed at the Old Bailey in 1981 for the murder of thirteen women.

While I was working on that case I picked up details of two other murderers who had killed their victims around the same time.

The Ripper case is probably the most notorious I have ever worked on and it brought me a certain amount of fame. After it was all over, the world famous sci-fi writer Arthur C. Clarke studied all the data given to the police by psychics – there were dozens of us working on the case – and he dismissed most of them. But he was impressed by what I came up with and even announced I was one of the world's great mysteries!

Right from the very start I never wanted to get involved with the Ripper. It is not that I am publicity shy; by then I was quite used to talking to reporters, and I was not afraid because it was such a big case. Only months before I had helped the police with the case of the Black Panther.

He was the man who murdered Manchester girl Leslie Whittle and left her body down a drain. On that occasion I had told the police that Leslie's body would be found down a drain. I even drew the drain for them.

But the Ripper case was different. Even before anyone contacted me about the murders I was picking up the feeling of the man, and that feeling was evil. Details of his crimes would flash before my mind at odd times during the day and I had the feeling I was close to him, but I would push the feeling away. I did not want to know this man. He frightened me.

One day in 1979 I was sitting at home having tea with Pamela, a local policewoman who is a friend of mine, when I felt as if a glass dome was being lowered over me and, in that dome, I was together with someone else. I know, without any shadow of a doubt, that I was with the Ripper.

He was a man completely consumed by the urge to kill. He was not insane, but he tried to excuse himself by saying he was on some kind of divine mission. He was saying he had messages from God telling him he had to kill prostitutes. (Eighteen months later it was strange to hear those very words come out at Peter Sutcliffe's trial at the Old Bailey.)

Suddenly, I saw the man walking by a cemetery; he was wearing a wind-cheater and carrying a bag, which I thought either carried his tools or his lunch. Then I saw him walking down a road and as I described the countryside he was looking at, Pamela jumped out of her chair.

'I know that place,' she said. 'It's in Yorkshire. It's not far from where I used to live.' The story of what I had seen appeared in a couple of newspapers and sometime later Shirley Davenport, a reporter who was working for the Yorkshire Post, phoned me. Could I come up with a more detailed description of the Ripper?

At that moment, a kind of booming noise echoed around the house, a man's face appeared in front of me and hovered just inches from my own. I yelled and dropped the phone. The man's face stayed staring at mine. He was so close I could see the perspiration on his forehead and smell his bad breath.

He sneered at me, but I could not look away from him. His eyes were magnetic.

I picked the phone up off the ground and slowly told Shirley what had happened.

'Is he still there?'

'Yes.'

'What does he look like?'

'He's older than the police think. There's a fine white line above his upper lip. I keep seeing an anchor – that might be a symbol. He might have something to do with water. But I keep being drawn back to his eyes. People always notice the eyes. I can't look any more.' I shut my eyes and tried to blank him out. I felt sickened to the core.

'He's going to kill again,' I told Shirley, 'and soon. And I think the next victim will be a youth. I can see a cap on his head and he's carrying a haversack. He's got short hair and he's wearing trousers.'

Outside it was a lovely summer's day but, at that moment, in my house, it was as cold as the coldest January day. At last the face faded away and I felt totally drained. But that night it returned and I could not sleep. Again and again, I saw the face.

By this time the Yorkshire Ripper was the most wanted man in Britain. He had killed eleven times and the police, it seemed, were no nearer finding him. But I was close to him, I had seen his face and I had seen into his mind. I had no alternative but to help as much as I could.

I suggested to Shirley that I would tell her as much as I could, some of which she could publicise but other things, which might encourage copy-cat crimes or interfere in any way with the police investigation, could be passed on to them for their eyes only. Shirley agreed and came over.

'I think I can tell you where he works and lives,' I told Shirley. 'I'm not much of an artist but I think I may be able to draw his face.'

I did not want to see that face ever again but I concentrated hard, using all the psychic power I could muster, to tune into the Ripper again.

There were some details which I was very sure of by then. I got Bradford very strongly. I was convinced he lived in Bradford and that he was a long distance lorry driver. I could see him driving all over the place. I saw him driving a red lorry and I thought it had something to do with engineering. I could see things that looked like reels of cable in the lorry.

I felt that if only I could go to Bradford, my gift would guide me to him. But what if he was away on one of his journeys?

By this time, I was almost becoming obsessed by the man. I had terrifying nightmares. In one, I was following the Ripper through the streets. Once, I saw the streets shining with rain; there was a cinema and a pub nearby, and he had parked his car. He was getting out of the car, staying in the shadows, and then he was following a woman as she walked up an alleyway. He was getting closer to her and I saw him raise his arm as if to strike her and then . . . the picture faded.

Another night, I saw him plunging a knife into a woman's body and I saw the initial 'A' so strongly. I thought maybe he carved an 'A' on the bodies of his victims just above the navel. The pictures kept coming until I was exhausted. Sometimes, I did not know if I was awake or asleep dreaming and, all the time, a feeling of dread was getting stronger and stronger.

Then in September 1979 a young student called Barbara Leach became the Ripper's next victim. As I read the details in the newspapers I felt sick. The description of Barbara was the same as the description of the youth I had given Shirley: cap, short hair, trousers and a sort of haversack.

The months passed and still the police had not caught him. I listened to the tape recording the police had made public from a man claiming to be the Ripper, but it did nothing for me. I phoned Detective Inspector Dave Pritchard, who had suggested I listen to the voice, and I told him 'I don't understand it. It's almost as if it's a different man. I get nothing from that voice.'

And I told Shirley, 'That man on the tape is not the man who committed all those murders.'

Some time later I held, in my hands, a photographed sample of a letter someone claiming to be the Ripper had written to the police. I was at home and I sat down by the coffee table in front of my fire, holding the letter. Voices echoed at me from every direction.

A voice shrieked 'Peter! Peter!'

Then I saw a little old man beside me who was practically bursting with fury and rage.

'Kill him!' he said. 'Kill him!'

I was being asked to kill Peter.

'But I can't kill him, I can't,' I cried.

Other voices told me to get a piece of paper and a pencil and soon I was drawing furiously: a flyover, a wide road, a lorry depot and big buildings which looked like chimneys. There was water, maybe a canal, behind the depot and I knew that on the left was the city centre.

Two street names seemed to be important – Charles Street and Chapel Street. It was Bradford; I was sure it was Bradford.

The clues were coming thick and fast now. I could see the man was working on his lorry. He had stopped at some kind of depot which he often visited. He was wearing overalls, but I knew that when he was not working he was a snappy dresser.

I could see there was a name written on the side of his lorry. I could not read all of it but I could see that the first letter was 'C', so he probably worked for a company beginning with 'C' – or was it just an advertisement the lorry carried? I could not be sure.

I kept getting the name Ainsworth, Ainsworth, Ainsworth. What was Ainsworth? Was it a name or a place? I was working on a sketch of the man's face. My voices guided me, 'No, the mouth's wrong, it needs to be a bit more like that,' or 'no, make the eyes bigger.' I kept listening and I kept working until I produced my sketch. It was no Picasso but the voices told me it was not a bad likeness.

Before Christmas, I kept getting the number six. What did that mean? Was that the number of his house or was that something to do with where the next murder would take place? Or did he live at 6, Chapel Street or Charles Street?

I cannot explain to you how frustrating it is when you get the clues but, instead of pointing you in one direction, they seem to lead you in a circle, around and around.

Soon the darkness and the feeling of dread descended on me again. 'He's going to kill again,' I told Shirley, 'And the next victim is going to be found on a small patch of waste ground.'

After that I felt I could not go on with the Ripper case. Physically it drained me, emotionally it terrified me. I really wanted nothing more to do with it. Shortly after I made this decision a woman's body was found, stripped and strangled, in the grounds of a house in Leeds. The house belonged to the chairman of the local magistrates, Mr Peter Hainsworth. So it was Hainsworth, not Ainsworth. But, then, I usually drop my aitches . . .

The police were convinced that this crime had nothing to do with the Ripper. Maybe they simply did not want to believe it but I knew it was him and, when he was finally arrested, he admitted to it, too.

In the Autumn of 1980 the now familiar fear swept over me again. I knew he was preparing to kill again, I could feel the urge building in him. I could see the initials of the victim – J H – but I could not see the name in full. I knew it would be Leeds and I had seen the wasteland where the poor girl's body would be found.

I saw a date – November 17 – or was it November 27? One of the two. The only thing that cheered me up was that I knew he was reaching the end of the road. He was going to be caught, not this time but certainly next.

The pictures that flashed into my mind were desperately depressing: the girl was lying half under some bushes or were they small trees? Her legs were sticking out. I felt that, perhaps, she had lost her shoe. She had dark hair. She was a nice girl. By now, he was killing indiscriminately, any young woman he could find. It did not seem to matter to him if they were prostitutes or not. What had happened to the voices from God, to his divine mission?

In fact, I have always believed that was nonsense, an excuse concocted afterwards, or maybe during his reign of terror, just to excuse his behaviour to himself.

On November 17 of that year, that wicked man killed Jacqueline Hill in Leeds.

I was asked to try and trace his steps after the murder and Shirley came with me up to Leeds and the scene of the crime. I felt strongly that this time he had made a mistake, left something behind, something on the ground. I walked up and down looking at the ground

While I was there I could feel the familiar presence of evil. By now I knew him, I knew his face.

'This is where he stood in the shadows waiting,' I told them and I knew there had been a struggle on the pavement, and the sound of snapping wood and twigs as he fell backwards onto a wire mesh fence. Then my feet followed his in the direction he made his escape. I knew what I was looking for. He had turned left, and then crossed the road – and there it was just a few hundred yards away – Chapel Street.

We drove down Chapel Street until we came to a station I had seen and described before from one of my visions. I knew he had left something here. We found it in the bushes; a rolled up bunch of newspapers. We did not touch it or unroll it, but passed it straight on to the police. They, in turn, held onto it as a possible exhibit and would not let me have it back. It was only weeks later that I discovered it was a roll of newspaper cuttings, most of them of naked women, or of a sexual nature, and, on one picture of a naked woman, there was a doodle of a matchstick man piercing the woman's heart with a knife.

Only a week after my trip to Leeds I had a crystal clear vision of where the Ripper worked. I was still convinced the place was something to do with engineering. It was a long low building with long windows and double doors near a canal.

Then something happened that terrified me. Even now, thinking about it makes a cold shiver run down my spine. The newspapers had been constantly recording my predictions and one reporter, who, incidentally I would personally like to throttle, printed my full address in the *Daily Mirror*. There it was – 'Amazing Predictions from Nella Jones of . . . Bexleyheath!'

I have always been scared that one day a criminal I was searching for would try and turn the tables and catch me as his next victim instead. I am quite sure that after Peter Sutcliffe read the story about me in the newspaper he set off to find me. Maybe he would not have hurt me, maybe he just wanted to talk to me. I will never know, but one thing I am sure of – he came to Bexleyheath to find me.

It was a Saturday and I was in the car with Albert, who, at that time, was the man in my life. We were just off to do some shopping. As we approached the end of the road I slammed on the brakes. A man had just walked past us.

I said, 'Do you see that man?'

Albert looked mystified. 'Yes. So?'

'That's the Ripper,' I said.

'You've got the Ripper on the brain,' he said.

Maybe he was right. But no, I thought, I felt it too strongly and my feelings about these things are rarely wrong.

Suddenly I knew that the Ripper had parked his lorry in Welwyn and got the train, or borrowed a car, to come down to Bexleyheath. By now we were in the car sitting in the middle of the road and the man was disappearing from view. So what was I supposed to do about it? The way I was feeling I did not want to do anything about it. Anyway, I reasoned, what could the police do? And they would probably think I was barmy . . .

But that night Pamela, my policewoman friend, popped around again after work.

'It's been a busy afternoon,' she said.

'Why, what's wrong?'

'We've had complaints from several women this afternoon who have been propositioned in the street by a man who suggested they were prostitutes. A man with a beard.'

Then she described him and I was shattered. It was him. The Ripper. The man I had drawn in my sketch.

I was jittery, to say the least. Shirley, the reporter, came down to look after me. I tried to see where the Ripper was as I spoke to her. It was cloudy at first but then, yes, there he was. He was sitting in a cafe drinking tea out of a white china cup and eating a chocolate éclair. I could see the pinball table in the cafe, a florists on one side of the cafe and an estate agent on the other. The Ripper was agitated, excited.

Just a few days before Christmas I kept getting the name Peter again, but I could feel the story was coming to a close. He would be caught very soon and I told my long-suffering family, who had probably been driven up the wall by my Ripper obsession for over a year, that I thought he was about to be caught and that we would hear good news on January 5.

In fact he was caught on January 3 although, at home, my family and I did not hear about it until the fifth. Apparently the police caught him in his car, after they became suspicious of the number plates on his Rover V8. In the car with him was a prostitute he had just picked up and, it goes without saying, that this girl had a very lucky escape.

Gradually all the facts emerged and, when I read accounts of the court case, even I was taken aback by the way all the clues in the jigsaw puzzle suddenly fitted together perfectly.

His name was Peter – Peter Sutcliffe. He was 35, older than the police had first thought. He lived at 6, Garden Lane. Was that why I had seen him in a landscaped garden? He was a long distance lorry driver and he did work for an engineering firm beginning with 'C'. Actually, they were called T W Clark but they had 'Clarks' written on the side of their lorries. He did live in Bradford, and he did kill Jacqueline Hill, initials 'J H', on November 17.

My drawing was not a bad likeness, in fact it was astonishingly accurate, and he had once worked as a gravedigger. Maybe that explained me seeing him in the cemetery. He had also once worked for the water board – did that explain my connection with water through the anchor? Or was that linked with the canal I kept drawing, because it turned out the firm he worked for was based in Canal Street? And their building was just as I had seen it in my head.

So I had done very well. But then, you might say, why didn't the police listen to me and simply interview all the long distance drivers in Bradford called Peter, who worked for an engineering firm beginning with the initial 'C'? Wouldn't that have saved many lives?

Unfortunately, it is not as easy as that, and I think it is worth noting here what I said earlier about other crimes which intruded on my vision during my trail of the Ripper.

These are the details I got wrong, at least these are the things I got wrong as far as the Ripper was concerned. But they proved uncannily accurate with other serious crimes being investigated around the same time.

Early on in the case I became very confused. I would see the Ripper's face and then his face seemed to change. I saw a younger man who was limping. He had something very wrong with one side of his body and I believed he had spent much of his childhood away from his natural family, maybe in a children's home. He, too, was consumed by some kind of unbalanced religious fervour but, in this case, I felt it was more genuine that that of the other older man. I got very strongly the name Dinsdale – a person or a place, I didn't know.

I usually saw the Ripper with a beard, but this other man had curlier hair. Could it be that there were two men committing these crimes? Peter was not the only name I had picked up during the investigation. When the old man came to me and said 'Peter' he then went on to say 'Charles' and a whole chorus of voices tuned in and started chanting 'Charlie is my darling, Charlie is my darling.'

And then the old man was jumping up and down shouting, 'Stop him, stop him.'

All of this made no sense at all and for a long time I was convinced the clues were all connected with the Ripper case, until the whole truth of that case was over and another case was in the papers.

In court, in 1981 in Leeds, close to where the Ripper had committed his crimes, a young man called Peter Dinsdale stood accused of murdering 26 people in six years of arson attacks. He pleaded guilty on the grounds of diminished responsibility.

To me, the facts of the case were quite extraordinary. He was paralysed down one side, he had spent years in a children's home and

45

he never stopped spouting fire and brimstone quotes from the Bible. What really chilled me was finding out that one of his victims, killed in the same month that the old man appeared to me, December 1979, was called Charlie.

Perhaps the old man was one of Dinsdale's elderly alleged victims or, perhaps, he was another relative of Charlie's who had passed to the other side.

There were other names I had picked up during the investigation too: I thought that Harry could have been the name of the Ripper's father, but it wasn't. But was it the name of another murderer's father? I also got the name Leonard very strongly, as well as many symbols which I wrote down at the time and which turned out to be Navy insignia. Could this man have been connected with a crime at the same time?

I have a strong feeling that this might have been the man who phoned the police claiming to be the Ripper and whose taped voice I had listened to. I can still see him in my mind, although I feel, by now, he might have passed over to the other side. He was a sad character, scruffy too. He liked to drink and bet on the dogs and I am sure the police, if they did but know it, were familiar with him. Of course he has a lot to answer for in making those hoax phone calls but I also feel he was somehow guilty of more than that . . .

So you can see, it is not always easy. Of course, it would be wonderful if I could solve any crime just by sitting here and shutting my eyes. But, maybe, I am not sufficiently psychically advanced myself to be able to do that and, anyway, the spirits who help me often feel that they are giving me enough clues to solve the crime. It is my fault if I do not interpret them correctly. I often feel that they are just as frustrated at my misreading of the clues as I am, when I look at what seems, at the time, an impossible puzzle.

Often I have to wait weeks, even months, before I discover how accurate my visions have been. Many facts about the crime and the criminal do not come out until the case reaches court. Then, it is extraordinary how little details I came up with, which apparently mean so little at the time, suddenly fit into the pattern with perfection.

At the time of writing I am still waiting to find out how accurate I was on the Stephanie Slater kidnap case earlier this year.

Stephanie, a young estate agent from Birmingham, was kidnapped in January as she showed a man around a house for sale. She was held for 10 days before being released after her firm paid a ransom of £175,000. After a massive manhunt, police finally arrested a man called Michael Sams, a 50-year-old engineer from Newark in Nottinghamshire. They also charged him with the murder of Julie Dart, a pretty teenager who was found dead in July 1991 in Lincolnshire, after disappearing from her Leeds home two weeks before.

I became involved, before Sams' arrest, after a newspaper

reporter called and asked me to see what I could do. First of all, I asked her to send me some maps of the area where all this had happened, especially the route the head of Stephanie's firm had taken as he dropped off the ransom money.

I often use maps. Usually, I do not actually read them. Instead, I run my hands over them and my hands are drawn to linger over one particular place.

A few years ago I was invited by a Japanese TV company to Osaka to attempt to solve some murders there and I used maps then very successfully – although the maps were complete gobbledegook to me as they were all written in Japanese!

On the Stephanie Slater case, the first thing I picked up was the name Michael and I got, very strongly, horses, the smell of horses. I was convinced that the man involved in the case was, somehow, connected with horses. I felt Stephanie would have been held in a horse box.

I got a farm and a barn – did the kidnapper live on a farm? I am still sure a barn was important in some way. When Sams was finally arrested I was surprised. I always believed this was not a case of one man working alone. I thought there were two people involved and, most probably, the second person was female. The police, however, have found no evidence to confirm this.

Sitting alone at home, the maps spread out on the dining room table, a lot of images started to flash into my mind. I got the name of a place called Frankley and a psychiatric hospital. A man involved in the case, I was sure, had some connection with a psychiatric hospital. But had he been a patient? Or had he worked in such a hospital? Or had he simply visited someone there?

I looked at the map and there were three hospitals all grouped together, so I called the reporter and asked her to check which one was a psychiatric hospital.

She quickly came back to me.

'All three,' she said. It was like looking for a needle in a haystack!

I closed my eyes for a while, then I got a piece of paper. Again, I had the urge to draw something. On these occasions I do not concentrate, I simply let my hands draw whatever they want to. I sketch the first thing that comes into my mind.

This time, I kept drawing an arrow head – not a whole arrow, not its shaft, just the arrow head. I looked at the map again to see if there was a field or anything like that shaped like an arrowhead. And that is when I saw a place called Arrowfield Top. Was that important? Had he been there?

I began to get a feeling of this man. I felt he had been remarkably lucky not to have been caught earlier. When the news first broke of Stephanie's kidnap, the first thing that came into my mind was, 'They'll have him within the week, they're very close.' But it was not until BBC TV's Crimewatch programme played a tape recording of the kidnapper's voice that a man was arrested.

At some point during their investigation I am sure the police were, quite literally, yards from their quarry. I have no doubt about that at all. Yet still they missed him.

The feeling I had from this man was very different from the feelings I got with the Ripper case. I did not feel this man was mad but I felt he had been very hurt by life itself. I thought 'Life has dealt this man a cruel blow or two.' I also felt pain in his back. I thought he suffered badly from a bad back.

But I did not feel that this man was a killer, so I was very surprised when I heard that they had also charged Sams with the murder of young Julie Dart. While I was working on the case I was convinced that another man had committed that crime. But only time will tell how my pieces of the jigsaw fit into the puzzle as a whole, if at all, and, of course, the guilt of Michael Sams still has to be established in relation to the kidnapping.

Just as I did not feel that the man who kidnapped Stephanie was a killer, there have been times when I have been sure that murderers who have been caught, and charged with the murder of one victim, are, in fact, guilty of killing many more. I am sure there are many more serial killers in this country, some in prison and others walking free, than is public knowledge. Often I know that the police know that the person they are holding for one crime is guilty of another. But, if they do not have the proof, or a confession, there is not much they can do about it. Sometimes, I can help them to make a connection between different crimes.

This happened only recently. A Detective Constable called Neil Pratt phoned me and asked if I could help him with a murder case that had remained unsolved for months.

A young woman had been found stripped and murdered in the early hours of the morning in Telegraph Hill Park, in Brockley, South London. They took me to the park and immediately a rush of images came through my mind. I knew this was a terrible crime and the man concerned was guilty, not just of this murder, but several more.

'This girl has just come back from Spain, Barcelona, I think,' I told Neil, 'and she has a child. I'm sure she has a child.'

In my mind I could see the girl travelling around. She was looking for somebody, somebody connected with transport. I could feel her obsession with a man; she was desperately in love with this man and she was following him around the country. It was a case of unrequited love but he was not the one who had murdered her.

I told Neil that I did not believe the girl had been raped.

'It was made to look like rape but it wasn't. She knew the man who killed her. She hadn't known him for long, but she had known him for a while. There's something missing from the scene of the crime, a piece of jewellery. He took a piece of jewellery from her.'

By now, the pictures were coming thick and fast. I could see a village near a river, and what looked like the New Cross area of South

London, but this murder had taken place miles away in Brockley.

Then I saw him as clear as day and, suddenly, I wasn't with the girl anymore. I was with the man who murdered her.

'He doesn't come from around these parts,' I told Neil. 'He was born further north in the Midlands and he is somehow involved in cars.'

As I felt I was getting closer to this man I also caught the scent of a strange smell, so strong that it stung my eyes. It was paint.

'I think he sprays cars with paint.' All the time I felt the man coming closer and closer.

'He's in his early thirties. In the past he's had some injury to the side of the head. He's still got the scar but you can't see it. He likes women, in fact he's obsessed with women, but what he likes best is to pick up a woman and drop her according to his own whim.'

'If a woman gets clingy, he gets rid of her, he won't see her any more. He's not mad but he is very dangerous.'

A few days later the police rang me back.

'Nella, if we show you a photograph of someone would you be able to say if he was the murderer or not?'

'I think so.'

A few hours later I sat in a little office in the police station with the photograph in my hand. I felt immediately that it was him. Worse, as I looked at him, I realised I had seen him before. No, we had never met, but this was the man I had seen when I was working on another case for the police three or four years earlier.

A young girl had been travelling on a train from London to Kent after a night out in town. She was found battered to death in the carriage. Her murderer had never been caught but, now, I felt I was looking at him.

At the time of the girl's murder I was asked by Chief Inspector Dave Morgan of Cannon Row police to help. It was a horrible case. I could see the girl in the carriage and she was talking to someone, another woman. She and this other woman were in the compartment alone. Quite naturally, they started chatting about everyday things. What the girl did not realise was that her companion was not a woman, but a man dressed in women's clothes.

I had told Dave, 'Don't look for a man – at least he is a man but you should look for a man who dresses as a woman.'

Now I believed I was looking at this man's face.

'I feel this is the man who killed the girl on the train,' I said. 'He's a transvestite.'

Then they told me that the man I was looking at was already in custody charged with the murder of another young girl.

'Where does he come from?' I asked them.

'The North,' they said. 'Yorkshire.'

'And does he have anything to do with cars?'

'He's very into cars. And he runs a spray-paint shop.'

Later they told me that they found out he had, indeed, been injured at one point on the side of his head although now no scar was visible. In his diary they had found the number for a transvestite club in London. If he didn't use that club, I asked, why did he carry around the number of the place?

I can picture the photograph of that man now and it still sends shivers up my spine. Other pictures came to me – another girl, her body limp in death, being carried. A lake. A splash, and she was gone. What did that mean? I still do not know.

All these crimes, all that suffering! As far as I know the police have never proved the connection but, in my heart, I am sure that somehow, in some way, they are linked. Maybe one day I shall be allowed to know the answer.

I could feel the evil in that man. He is not mad. He is plain evil and, remember, there are evil people on this earth just as there are good ones. They love doing evil, they love it, they enjoy killing. Sometimes, when I work on a case I can feel their enjoyment in it. It is sick, horrific, and I always feel I don't want to get involved in this, but I know I have to if I am going to find out anything.

I feel a whole bundle of emotions that are completely foreign to me and that is the most stressful part of it. *I* do not have those feelings, they are not *my* emotions. I do not enjoy evil; I do not enjoy killing, I am just an ordinary woman, but I can feel all that they feel. I feel the fear *they* feel when they kill, but the fear is part of the excitement for them.

Even on robbery cases I feel the robbers' fear. But I also sense adrenalin rushing through them; simultaneously with the fear there is the thrill of 'living life on the edge'. It is a formidable combination. But I cannot let the fear get to me. I mustn't, I would never be able to do anything if I let the fear get to me.

Sometimes, I also feel what the policemen on the case are feeling. I can't help but pick it up and, in some strange way, it is similar. There is fear – particularly on a murder case when they know most of the gory details which the public do not. And there is always the fear that the murderer is going to murder again and again. There is anxiety, pressure, but sometimes I also pick up their excitement in the chase. That is not to say they in any way enjoy the murder, or are not horrified by what some human being has brought himself to do to another. But it is only human for the drama of it all to get to them. And, through them, to me.

I am often asked how I get on with the police, and, I suppose, my relationship with them is a strange one in many ways. Some of the coppers I know have become good friends, others view me with great suspicion. A few actively disapprove of me and my psychic work. I can sense that.

They are not only sceptical, they are very 'anti' what I do. I can read their minds as they are sitting there. Maybe a superior officer has called me in, the officer I am seeing who, personally, thinks it is a daft idea but he has to put up with it, and I can sense that he is almost disappointed when I get things right!

But, increasingly, most policemen keep an open mind. If they are up against a brick wall in a case, they are prepared to try almost anything and I genuinely do not believe it is just because they want their own career records to look good. They genuinely want to catch villains. It is their job and most of them take a pride in that job and want to do it well. Many of the policemen are like the people who come to me for healing. They think it probably won't work, but they have tried everything else, they have got nothing to lose and it will not cost them anything. So why not? I am usually the last resort when they are clutching at straws. And I am a very good straw!

I have never received anything from the police in return for the help I have given them. If I am lucky they say 'thank you' and if I am very lucky I work with an officer who has the decency to ring me and tell me the end result of a case. It is terribly frustrating when I am not told how right or wrong I was.

But I have never had any payment, no expenses, not a bean. I don't mind really. Often, when I am drained and exhausted, or tramping through fields looking for clues, or sitting sleepless in the middle of the night working on a case, I say to myself, 'Nella, what the hell are you doing this for?'

I suppose the only answer is that I do not have a choice. It is my duty. That may sound pompous but that is, honestly, how I feel. If I have this gift, if I can see things that help to put these people away where they can't do any more harm, then I have to use it.

Mind you, I have thought more than once, particularly when I have been on my uppers, that a little of the reward money would not have gone amiss.

I remember one night when Greenwich police came to see me. There had been a bank robbery at Barclays Bank and what the police wanted to know was where the thieves had stashed the money. As soon as the CID man started speaking I could see the raid, I could see the guns the robbers were carrying, how they got in and how they got out. It was like looking at a video in my head.

I saw them make off with the money. They put it all in a kind of holdall and hid it in a lock-up garage by the waterfront in Greenwich. I described the place and the surroundings in detail, although I was not sure exactly where the place was.

Anyway, the police searched the waterfront and there was the money in the holdall in the lock-up, just as I had described.

When one of the police officers was good enough to ring and tell me how right I had been I could not resist the temptation.

'There was quite a reward on that job, wasn't there?' I said. 'Where do I pick it up?'

'Sorry Nella,' he replied with a chuckle, 'the chief says we got the information from a man in a pub.'

If I have heard that once I have heard it a million times! It really is quite extraordinary how so many men, in so many pubs, so often give such useful information, to so many policemen!

Some of the policemen I meet sometimes become friends. I can be sitting at home doing something quite ordinary like the washing up, when I pick up pictures of what a criminal is up to, but sometimes I also suddenly tune into moving pictures starring officers I have worked with.

I first met Detective Inspector Don Middleton at Belvedere police station in South London. I had gone there to help out on another case, the suspicious death of an old lady.

Don was also working on an entirely different case. We passed the time of day and as we sat chatting the old familiar flashes started. Without thinking I looked at Don and said, 'You're going to go to a caravan site and you're going to go up to a little white caravan and you're going to arrest somebody.'

He nearly fell out of his chair. Then he said, 'Where's the caravan site?'

So I described the site to him, the caravan and where it was and he gave a big grin, 'So that's where I'll find my man, will I?'

After that little episode I went with Don to the house where the old lady had died. We had not worked together before, but he was open-minded and grateful for anything I could tell him. I was on form that day. I could see everything that had happened, but it was another nasty case.

It was a break-in and I told him how the man had got in. By the front door a glass panel had been smashed in but I said to Don, 'He did not come in that way, he came in the back.' I could see the place where the old lady had fallen and I told him what the man had done to her. No doubt because of the way she was handled, she had a heart attack and died in hospital two days later, poor old soul. I knew it was a local person and I was able to tell Don that someone else had evidence against the murderer which would finally convict him. Most of it worked out as I had said and they got the murderer, which is the most important thing.

After that I did not speak to Don for a long time until, one day, he turned up on the doorstep with his wife. He had never been to my house before and it was just a social call to begin with, although, in the end, it turned out to be business as well.

As I have said before, pinpointing the exact time of any event is hard. Yesterday, today, tomorrow? Sometimes I just don't know.

As we were chatting away I said to Don, 'By the way, that murder case you're working on, that lady was not murdered where she was found. She was murdered somewhere else. She came from the Midlands, she was killed there.'

'You've got it all wrong this time, Nell,' he said. 'I'm not working on any murder case.'

'Oh,' I said, 'sorry about that.' Well, I'm not right all the time . . .

The next morning Don went into his office and there was a report on his desk about a woman who had been murdered. She was from the Midlands, it read, but she had been found murdered in a derelict building in London. The pathologist's report in the next envelope stated quite clearly – the woman was not murdered where she was found, she was murdered elsewhere, and her body had merely been dumped in London.

It was another eighteen months before I heard from Don again and then it happened in a most extraordinary way. I was at home one morning when I suddenly felt I was with him again, and I heard a young girl say to him, 'Daddy why can't I have a pony, why can't I have a horse?'

I finished my chores and got on the phone to Don, who was surprised to hear from me after so long.

'Don Middleton,' I said. 'Why don't you buy that horse your daughter wants?'

There was a silence, then he roared with laughter.

'You were in the car with us this morning, were you?'

'Don't be silly, of course I wasn't.'

'Well, you might as well have been. I was driving her to school when, for the first time, she asked if she could have a pony. Do you know how much they cost? I quickly changed the subject!'

We had a good laugh about it. Don is one of the nicest police officers I have ever known. In fact, most of them are a decent bunch. I haven't met many I didn't like.

They don't come around to my house every Friday any more. I had to put a stop to that because if I started to get involved in every crime that every policeman I knew was involved in I would never stop. I couldn't cope with it. It would be too much pressure. I would end up going right round the bend. But, I am happy to help when I can.

I have no complaint against the ordinary rank and file police officers, the CID, the ones on the ground who are actually doing the work. It is some of their bosses who annoy me. Many of them are terrified to admit that psychics like me help in investigations.

But why? What is so frightening about admitting it? And what on earth is wrong with turning to a psychic for help? The most important thing is that they catch these wicked people and put them behind bars so they can't hurt anyone else. If I can help them find the proof, why not use me?

Not so long ago a Chief Superintendent from Scotland Yard rang me up and said he wanted to see me and to record the details of all the cases I had worked on. I was not sure why they wanted to do this but I agreed. He came to visit me in Bexleyheath.

I told him everything and, I could tell, he was quite impressed. He even thanked me for all the help I have given the police over the years and he was contacted when I appeared on the James Randi TV show – he is the magician who makes a career out of trying to prove that anything psychic or paranormal is a load of old nonsense.

Yet, even after his visit, all the Chief Inspector could say to Randi, was that there was no written evidence that I had ever helped the police in any way. He did not actually say he had never met me, but that was the impression he gave.

I was very hurt by that and, more, I was angry. It made me out to be a liar, which I am not. What are they so afraid of? Are they worried that the public will think our police force is no good because, occasionally, they get stuck and turn to psychics for any help we can give? I do not believe that the majority of people are that narrow-minded any more.

There are some policemen who have the courage to admit that they know me, and have worked with me, and to them I am grateful. As for the others, no comment.

THREE

The Healing Touch

'I went to Nella three years ago with a bad backache. I had been suffering pain for several years due to a prolapsed disc, which means a disc that has slipped out between the spinal segments.

'I felt nothing out of the ordinary, there was no electric shock or anything like that when Nella laid her hands on my back. But one hour later the pain had gone and, apart from the odd small twinge, I haven't been in pain since.

'It is true to say that I had visited an osteopath some time before so, maybe, it was half osteopath and half Nella, but the pain only left me after I had visited her.

'After that I took her to see a patient of mine who was suffering from cancer and was in great pain and, after Nella had touched her, her pain was eased considerably.

'I don't believe that people who go to psychic healers are necessarily hysterical or barmy. In my case it was "any port in a storm" and it worked.

'An individual's response to pain is very difficult to judge and we do not fully understand what the human mind is capable of. In my case I certainly don't feel it was simply mind over matter. I don't believe it worked merely because I thought it would. I wasn't sure whether it would work or not but I was willing to try it.

'I cannot explain what happened. I am a doctor but I believe one should keep an open mind.'

DR. DAVID WEDDERSPOON, LEYBOURNE GENERAL
HOSPITAL,
WEST MAWLING, KENT. MARCH 1992

'When I first met Nella I really was in quite a state. I had already had two operations for cancer of the colon and then they discovered a huge ulcer to one side of my stomach.

55

The surgeon couldn't remove it so he did an operation which cut off my digestive system.

'I had never been to a psychic healer before but in the months after the operation I felt so awful and was in such pain that I remember thinking that I wished I knew of one because I couldn't go on like this. The doctors had done their best but there was little they could do to help me further. Then by chance a friend told me about Nella.

'The first time she came to see me I lay on the bed and she ran her hands down the length of my body and along my arms. Not much more than that really. While she was doing it I felt very calm and very floppy. She told me I wouldn't feel any different for a couple of days and after a few days the pain did start to ease.

'Since then she has healed me over the phone. When I am in pain I ring her and she tells me to place my hands over various parts of my body.

'When she first did it she told me I would see a light on my hand and suddenly I did see a little white light on my hand as if someone was shining a pencil torch on me. Over the months the light changed colour from white, to pink, to a dark colour, like a bruise.

'It sounds barmy but my family have seen it too and I can assure you it's there. Now, whenever I phone Nella, as soon as she says "hello" the dark light appears on my hand. It is quite incredible. She gives me the treatment and I hold my hand over various places and she always says to me, "The pain will be gone by tomorrow darling." In fact it goes as I am talking to her. A couple of hours later it may come back a little but hardly at all and the light usually stays on my hand for a couple of hours.

'I rang her every night for four or five months. Now I ring her once a week. She has made such a difference to my life. After the operation I had adhesions and they were dreadfully painful but Nella got rid of them in four weeks.

'The doctors can't give me painkillers because my body can't take them after my operations and I don't know what I would have done without Nella. She has helped me so much. One very extraordinary thing happened after I first saw her.

'After she left, I saw a pale blue ribbon tied around my waist and I felt as if this ribbon led all the way to where Nella was. It's really most peculiar. I told her about it later and she wasn't surprised. She said, "Oh most people see silver chains that go from them to me."

'I never used to be a great believer in faith healing or psychic healing or whatever you want to call it.

'When the light first appeared on my hand I thought I was imagining it, but whichever way I turned my hand it was still there and my family saw it too, so I realised it must be true.

'You cannot say that what Nella does for me is "mind over matter". If it was, how do you explain the light? I think she's a wonderful woman and the way she eases my pain is just marvellous.

'My doctor says it's a miracle.'

MAVIS MOTT, 70,
HYTHE, KENT. MARCH 1992

When I was a child, and we were living in the village of Eynsford, a lovely mancalled Charlie Meadows lived down the road. His name suited him. His face was like a weathered rock and he had that ruddy glow about him which people seem to get when they spend most of their working life outside in the fresh air.

I have no idea how old Charlie was. He had white whiskers and he always seemed very old to me as a child! He had been a shepherd for most of his life and he lived in a small hut. All the kids loved him. He was one of those people who, after just five minutes, make you feel you have known them all your life and, to us, he was one of the few grown-ups you could talk to with ease.

Charlie loved animals, he had a way with them, and whenever we found a creature out in the fields which was injured or sick we would pick it up and gently carry the casualty to Charlie's hut.

One day we found a mole, by the roadside, which was obviously hurt. My friend picked it up and we set off to find Charlie with an absolute faith that he would know what to do with it.

'What's the matter with it, Charlie?' said my friend.

'It's very poorly,' he said.

'What are you going to do with it, Charlie?'

'I'm going to give it to Nella,' he said. 'She'll make it better.'

Strangely enough that did not surprise me at all. That is just what I had expected him to say. He gave me the little creature and very gently I held it in my hands and loved it.

Within a few minutes it wriggled and opened its eyes and we could see it was healed. Charlie looked at me and smiled. I don't know how he knew that I had the gift, but he did, maybe simply because he had it too so he recognised it in me.

While I was holding that mole, I loved it with all of me. You have to love them. That is the whole secret of all healing. You have got to love whatever you are healing whether it is an animal or a human being.

You either have got that love inside you or you haven't. You can't cultivate that kind of love on the spot, you have got to be born with an outgoing love for everything else, for every living thing around you.

A few days later some children found a sparrow which was injured, probably the little thing had fallen out of its nest.

Charlie wasn't around so they brought it to me and said, 'Nella, will you hold it for us?' I did, and it got better.

All I did was cradle it in my hands and the feeling I had then, for that sparrow, is just the same as the feeling I have these days when I am healing someone with migraine, or a frozen shoulder, or even cancer.

It is a difficult feeling to describe but I can try. When I am healing I feel all the love of my being going out to that person. I can feel energy inside me and then I can feel the energy leaving me and entering the other person. I know it is going into them. I can almost see it and, if I have a long session, healing many different people, I am literally drained at the end of it.

But it's always the same feeling whoever I am healing.

After Charlie gave me the mole to heal, I healed all kinds of creatures. Even when most of the children in the village weren't speaking to me because their parents had said I was a witch, they still brought me their injured pets. And even when I felt lonely because they wouldn't let me play with them, I never turned them away. I have never been able to turn anyone away.

I was much older when I started to use my gift to heal people. When I was seventeen and living with Eric and little Eric in London, a neighbour I was talking to told me she suffered terribly from migraine.

I felt very sorry for her so without thinking I said, 'Why don't you sit down for a minute?'

I put my hands gently on her head and the same old feeling came over me and within minutes her headache was gone. Of course, she told her friends, and they told their friends, and soon dozens of them were turning up on the doorstep with all sorts of complaints. One even had a thrombosis in her leg and that cleared up.

It was strange how it worked out. People would turn up almost every day for six weeks and then, suddenly, there would be nobody. It was as if I was being allowed some time off! Then, after a break, when I felt more rested, another batch of people would begin to arrive.

I didn't deliberately set out to heal. I didn't go into it with any kind of plan or purpose in mind and I have never advertised. All the hundreds of people who have come to me for healing have heard of me by word of mouth. It is as if I have healed those I am meant to heal.

I think, for it to work, my kind of healing must be natural. I have never met anyone who has actually been trained as a spiritual healer and most of the healers I have known started healing instinctively at a very early age.

I do have one young man working with me now who wants to be a healer. He is aware of a 'love feeling' for the patients. He has watched me work and he has sensed the healing atmosphere in the room – everyone senses it – and now he is having some measure of success.

But whether he will ever become a true healer I don't know. I hope so. We need more healers in the world, we need them desperately.

I have had journalists and TV camera crews sitting in on my healing sessions, some of them very sceptical, some of them not, and all of them trying to make sense of it.

I think the TV presenter Kevin Cosgrove summed it up when he came down with the BBC Nationwide team to film a healing session in my house. It was a very heavy session, the house was packed and at the end of the broadcast, he looked into the camera and said, 'Well, you can see how many people are here and, whether you believe in it or not, these people must get something out of it because Nella doesn't charge for this.'

And I don't. I have never charged for healing and I never would. I believe I am doing God's work. I have always had a deep faith in God. When I was little we didn't go to church and no one ever made me say my prayers. But, even as a tiny tot, I prayed. I prayed to Him and to Jesus. I don't know how I knew about God but I seemed to know a lot about Him. It was as if I was born with all that knowledge already there inside me. Maybe, in different ways, we all are.

I couldn't charge for healing because I couldn't live with the guilt. I would feel very ashamed because, whatever it is that God gave me from the beginning of my life, it is a gift from Him. If I asked people for money for healing I would be selling God's gift and you must never do that.

I have no idea why God gave me this gift. Sometimes I think perhaps that this is my life's work, that healing is the only reason I am here at all. But why did He pick me? I don't know. Maybe I didn't have much else 'between the ears' so, instead, He said, 'give her this gift.'

I have learned in life – I have *had* to learn in life – that there are many things you cannot explain, things that you just have to open your heart to and accept.

Years ago, when Gaynor and I were living on our own in the flat, I had a business appointment in Charlton but, because I was early, I had some time to kill so I wandered around the shops.

I felt myself drawn to a junk shop and went in. It had some nice antique pieces on display but most of the stuff was bric-a-brac. I didn't know what I was looking for. In fact I hadn't been intending to buy anything. I could not afford it for one thing! But I knew I would know what I was looking for when I had found it!

It turned out to be a battered high stool. Not antique, not valuable, not even particularly attractive. The wood was dark and it had a white leather seat but, as soon as I saw it, I knew I had to have it. I thought, 'That will do for my healing sessions. They can sit on that.' And I've used that stool ever since.

I put the stool in the middle of the room and people sit on it, unless their problem is back pain in which case they stand while I heal them. The stool is quite old and battered by now – an awful lot of people have sat on it – but I would not part with it for the world.

I give healing sessions at home every week and sometimes I see as many as thirty people. I always know when I have to stop. I get too tired and then I am no help to anyone.

I heal people individually, but we are not alone, other patients sit around. The room can be crammed, but it does not bother me. I don't see the other people. Even when an entire TV crew have been here with all their big lights and paraphernalia it hasn't distracted me.

I do not think about them. My whole concentration is on my

patient who is sitting on the stool. Everything else is dim; near, but far at the same time, blocked out.

Sometimes people will not tell me what is wrong with them. Sometimes I know they are thinking, 'She's the healer – let her tell me.' But that does not bother me either. I do not care what they are thinking.

Often I do not even know their names and frequently I forget what they have said to me, or I to them, immediately after the healing.

If the patient has not told me what the problem is I run my hands over them and I might say, 'You have got a problem here,' or 'There is a bit of trouble there.' When I reach that part of the body my hands stop as if they had a life of their own. They just will not let me go any further. I can just sense that there is something there that shouldn't be there.

With patients who have bad backs, or painful arms and shoulders, the healing is very fast. I do it quickly. Sometimes I pace up and down for a few minutes, and then I feel the energy building up in me. I run my hands over the place where the problem is, or just lay my hands on the body, and the healing is finished and the feeling goes.

Sometimes there is no reaction in the patient at all, but most of them say they feel some sort of heat in their body, a bit like the warmth you get from those eucalyptus creams that sports people use on strained muscles.

Other get a tingly feeling, a little like pins and needles, and quite a few feel dizzy when they stand up. No one has ever recoiled from the feeling. They say it feels strange, but it is also a pleasant sensation. I myself just feel drained and thank God if it has worked. And, when it has worked, I have never had anyone come back to see me to say, 'Nella, this complaint is back again.'

I know that many people in the medical profession think that healers such as myself cannot do any good. But, equally, there are others who not only think we do have a role to play, they even come to us themselves.

I have treated several doctors. I treated a senior doctor from Guy's Hospital in London who had the most horrific psoriasis all over him but nothing would heal it. I healed him here at home and then did other sessions at his house and fortunately it cleared up.

One doctor who comes to me for healing is Dr Wedderspoon of the West Mawling Hospital. He's a big man, a very sweet and clever man. His wife used to come to me for clairvoyance. He suffered terribly from a bad back and none of his colleagues could help him so she sent him along to me and his back was been improving ever since.

Afterwards Dr Wedderspoon asked me to heal a patient that he and the other doctors could not help. One Sunday he came and picked me up and took me down to Gillingham in Kent to see an old lady called Edith. I think he had known her since he was a young man.

When we got to the house, there was this poor old lady lying in bed in a tiny bedroom. She was in so much pain she could not move, even moving her head was absolute agony for her. Her sister was there looking after her and there were a couple of neighbours who had come in.

Usually I don't mind people around when I am healing but, this time, I felt I had to be alone with Edith. It was terrible to see someone in such pain. She was absolutely rigid.

Her bed was narrow and it did not face the door but was placed alongside an opposite wall. She could not even turn her head to see who was coming into the room.

I sat with her for a while, then I laid my hands on her head. Slowly, I ran my hands down her body. I was hardly touching her because even the gentlest touch gave her pain.

'How do you feel sweetheart?' I said.

'I feel a kind of tingling all over,' she said.

'That's great.'

I went and opened the door and said to the others, 'You can come in now.'

She turned her head towards them and smiled at them.

'This is fantastic,' she said.

I could see the astonishment on Dr Wedderspoon's face.

I said, 'I think she could drink another cup of tea now, couldn't you Edith?'

She said she would love one. Then she started pushing herself back in the bed and sitting up. I don't think she realised even then what had happened.

Her sister said, 'Edith, look at you!'

'What?' said Edith.

'You're sitting up.'

'Oh God, so I am,' she said.

The tears came into her eyes and soon she was crying and her sister was crying. It was all terribly emotional. Of course, for me, when anything like that happens, it is very, very rewarding. When I witness such healing I always feel very humble and I think, 'My God, what a responsibility you've given me.' It is daunting.

Dr Wedderspoon drove me home. I felt very tired afterwards and the next day he rang to say that Edith was now out of bed and walking around the house.

One of my favourite patients was a beautiful little baby boy who was just over two years old. One of his legs was completely normal but the other was badly deformed. He had been born with no knee joint, just a foot at the end of the thigh bone.

The doctors were thinking about amputating his foot but, before they did that, his parents decided to bring him along to me. I began to heal him every week. After a while his X-rays showed a knee joint and the rest of the leg was beginning to grow. His leg was actually growing! His parents were over the moon.

People who do not believe in the power of healing will always say that the healer has nothing to do with the healing. They say that if you believe in something strongly enough, if you have enough faith, then it will work. I think there is some truth in that – but only to a certain extent.

It does not explain what happens with the little babies, the small children, the animals. I didn't explain to the little boy what I was doing. Ho do you explain healing to a two-year-old? I could sense he trusted me but he really did not know what was going on. Faith in my ability to heal him had nothing whatsoever to do with it. It couldn't have.

Of course, there are so-called healers who are confidence tricksters and get the rest of us a bad name. I have heard all kinds of stories about people who profess to do psychic surgery where, using the hands alone, they actually enter the body and operate and there is not even a scar to show what they have done.

I don't believe I could do that, but I do believe psychic surgery can work. It is such a fantastic phenomenon that it is difficult to believe in it, but I am sure it's possible. The only problem with all this, of course, is that there are so many clever frauds. People think, 'Right, we can cash in on this,' and they do.

A psychic surgeon would have to be someone with extraordinary psychic power. They must be very rare, and if you ever come across one taking payment for what he does, walk away. True healers, especially one of such talent, could not take money for healing.

Most of our healing sessions at home are quiet affairs. People stand around chatting while someone like my friend Thelma ushers the patients up to me one by one to sit on the stool. Sometimes it is almost like a conveyor belt! One sits on the stool and I heal, then they get off and someone else gets on. I hardly know who has come and gone.

One night a young girl of about eleven sat on the stool. The poor thing had a terribly big goitre on her throat. It looked horrible and a complaint like that is very upsetting, especially for someone of that age. I did not know the goitre was supposed to be inoperable. I just gave healing in my normal way and she got off the stool, then an old man got on it, and then someone else.

Suddenly I heard a great commotion outside in the hall. I thought, 'What's going on?' and everything stopped. The people who had brought the girl said, 'Look!' The goitre had gone.

The girl was thrilled to bits but I learned later that her parents were absolutely furious because it was a neighbour who had brought her along without their knowledge. They said that healing was witchcraft and a load of mumbo-jumbo so they were livid – even after they saw she had been cured.

There was another very strange incident at the house the night the Nationwide TV crew was here. I was by the stool and, suddenly, I was conscious of a young man standing by the light switch. I had never met him before, I didn't even know his name.

He told me he had a frozen shoulder. His arm was stiff and he could not raise it. So I healed him and he said it was fantastic, he could move his arm and the pain had gone. He kept saying, 'This is really remarkable.' Then he left and I thought no more about him.

Later on in the session the phone rang and it was the same young man. He wanted to speak to the television people and, when they went to the phone, he said, 'Look, I've got to tell you. What Nella didn't know when I came down was that I was blind in one eye. Now I can see out of that eye again!'

The man had never mentioned his eyesight to me while I was healing him and, during the healing, I did not pick it up. But I think when you are being healed you get a measure of healing all over your body not just in the part you believe is sick or injured.

Some cases are much more difficult than others and I would not ever pretend that I can cure everybody of every ailment. Mental illness is the most difficult of all. I have worked on some chronic nerve cases but I am not always successful. I'm not sure why. Perhaps it is because the brain itself is such a complex organ, there are so many parts of it to be healed or restored.

Treating cancer is also very difficult. When I am healing someone with cancer I feel different. It is harder. It is much more difficult to pour your energy and love into that person. You feel as if there is an invisible barrier there stopping you, but eventually, hopefully, you can get through it.

I have got one cancer patient at the moment, a lovely lady called Mavis, who is married to a newspaper man and lives in Hythe in Sussex. When I was first asked to go and see her she looked as if she was literally on her death bed, the poor thing. She could not eat, she could only manage fluids and she was as thin as a bean.

I went up to her bed and I gently ran my hands down the length of her body.

'It's a fantastic feeling,' she said, 'I feel warm and comfortable all over.'

I knew she needed more healing than I could give her in that amount of time, but there was a problem – I could not afford to keep travelling all the way down to Hythe, but I was determined not to take any money from her.

But the answer came to me. I said to Mavis that she was to phone me every night at eight o'clock. She agreed and the next night the phone rang right on time. Over the phone I told her, 'Now, take your right hand and place it there. Now place it there. Now move it there. And you're going to see a light on your hand.'

She told me that she had started to see a light on her hand but I thought she might think that the light was merely some kind of auto-suggestion so I said, 'It's not a normal light, is it Mavis?'

64

'No,' she said. 'It's very dark. It's like a beam of dark light shining on my hand.'

That might sound a contradiction but I knew what she meant. Of course only Mavis saw the light that time because she was in a room by herself telephoning me.

Next I said to her, 'OK Mavis, now we're going to start transmitting the energy, let's hope we get it.' I healed her over the phone, and while I was healing she saw the light the entire time. I knew she would, I don't know how, but I knew. I have done quite a lot of healing over the phone but not to such an extent that the light was transmitted.

Mavis phoned me every night and soon her husband saw the light. He would not believe it until he saw it with his own eyes. Then the rest of her family saw the light, and her neighbours.

I think the light is a concentrated force of energy which passes from me to Mavis; the thoughts are going from me to her. I believe all our thoughts have to go somewhere, they cannot be lost. Who knows where most of them go? But I know where they go when I am healing – they go into my patient.

Mavis is now eating well, she has been on holiday to Norfolk to see her children, she is a different woman. Now, she only needs to ring me once a week and she often says to me, 'Nella, before you came along I knew I was dying, I knew it.'

She has had several big operations for cancer; they have taken nearly all of her stomach away, but she is doing fine. Even her doctor has said to her, 'How's your healer, Mavis? I hope you're keeping up with the sessions.'

And when she tells him she is, he says, 'Good. You're doing remarkably well.'

For many people who are sick I am the last resort. Many of them have been all through the medical system until the doctors have had to tell them there is nothing more they can do. So they come to me. I am the last hope.

I would guess that about fifty per cent of people who come to me actually believe that the healing is going to work. The others think, 'Well, I'll try it. What have I got to lose?' It does not cost them anything and it cannot hurt them.

Some of my patients are not even Christians, they are aetheists. They have often said to me, 'I have no faith, Nella. I don't believe in God.'

I say, 'Well, don't worry, I've got enough for both of us.' It doesn't actually bother me what faith they have. I have always had a strong faith, I go to church occasionally when I can and I pray often, every day, every night. I am always talking to Him. Whenever the need arises, I have a chat with The Governor.

I often pray at night-time or in the early morning when the world is quiet. I talk to God as if I were talking to you, I communicate in the same way, and sometimes, if I've done a healing session and I am not happy about one particular person, I will say something like, 'Well, Boss, this one's not too well. I'm not happy about this person and I feel there's something more extensive there that I'm not picking up. So help me, give me that extra strength to find out what it is and to help me clear it up.'

And I often add, 'God, be with him or her tonight.'

I heal Muslims, Jews, anyone of any faith. I strongly believe in one God and people have often said to me, 'But how do you relate the healing you do to God and Christianity?'

I say, 'Look, imagine life as a mountain and we have to reach that peak which is God. We all go up that mountain by our own path, we all have a different route, but we all get to the same place in the end.'

Sometimes, when I am healing, I hear God's voice. Last year a little girl was brought to me by her parents and grandparents. She had Wheels Cancer. I had never heard of it before but, apparently, it is a very rare and severe form of cancer. She had been in Great Ormond Street, the famous London hospital for sick children. They had taken a kidney out and found cancer in her lungs and she was only seven years old, the poor little thing.

Her name was Alison and the doctors had said that there was really nothing more they could do to save her, so the family brought her to me. I was their last hope.

She would come in and I would say, 'Any pain this week, poppet?'

She would reply, 'I've got a pain in my head' or 'I've got a pain in my tummy.'

Then I'd say, 'Well, let's get rid of this pain then,' and I would start to work on her.

I did all the healing I could, just laying on hands as I always do, giving out as much love as I could. Then, one week when she was with me, as I was laying my hands on her head, I felt another pair of hands fall gently over mine and I knew. I heard a voice saying, 'This one is mine, Nella.'

I knew from that moment that I was not going to save her and that she was going to die very soon. I did not tell her parents but I think they knew too. But, if I could not save her, I also knew that there was one thing I could do, and that was to keep her free of pain until the end.

That is just what I did. I had told her parents, right from the word go, that I could only do my best. I always say to everyone, 'I'm making no promises,' and that's what I told this family.

But this time I added, 'But should the worst come to the worst, I'll be here for you as well.'

I never built up their hopes but they could see that I was able to keep Alison free of pain and I hope, with all my heart, that was some comfort to them as well as her. Two weeks later I went to the little mite's funeral. A child's funeral is a terrible experience.

Afterwards I received the most moving letter I have ever been sent. Her parents wrote, 'Dearest Nella, We shall be eternally grateful for all you did for Alison and the love and care you showed her. You were there when no other help was there.' I cannot repeat more of the letter because it is so personal to Alison's parents, but every time I read it, I cry, and every time I think of Alison, I cry. She was such a beautiful child, and so young. But it was God's will – and that is tough at times.

About six years ago, on a Tuesday evening, I looked around my house during one healing session and thought, 'This is getting ridiculous.' The place was absolutely crammed. There were people sitting everywhere, up the stairs, in the hall, in all the rooms, all waiting to be healed. So I decided the time had come to start doing healing sessions in halls. That way, I thought, I could help many more people.

Healing in a hall is no different from the way I do it in my own home. I heal some people individually, one by one, sitting on my stool. I always take my stool with me. But then I ask the whole congregation to pray for the other people in the audience, people who need help, and I feel the same feeling.

I am healing 'en masse' and I can really feel that the prayers of all the other people in the audience are helping me. If I am up on the stage and I look out at a sea of faces in the audience, I can immediately recognise the people who need healing.

Sometimes I see a light surrounding them, sometimes, for no paticular reason, I seem to be drawn to one person. It is a strange sensation but I trust my instincts; I trust the gift I have been given, and it has very rarely let me down.

Just as I accept there are some things I cannot understand but must accept, so there are rules I follow when I am healing which no one ever taught me but which I know to be true. For example, I know that my right hand is positive and my left hand is negative.

I would never use my right hand in trying to heal anything with heart problems. I would not risk a positive charge going through the heart because it is too powerful. I have always known that from the earliest days of my healing. It is a knowledge that has always been with me.

I had to give up healing in halls because I couldn't charge admission and, in the end, I couldn't afford the hire fees. But I heal frequently at home, usually two or three times a week, sometimes more.

I wish I could say that I always enjoy it, or that I always look forward to it. To be honest, brutally honest, I don't.

It is just something I know I have to do. At first, when I was little, it was the animals. Then, after I started to heal people from the age of seventeen, there never seemed to be any lack of patients. There were neighbours and friends, and friends of friends.

When I was living on the caravan site and the boys were young, word got around and people used to queue outside for me to heal their aches and pains. When I lived with Ben we did not get on with his family, but still everyone else in the yard came to me when they were feeling poorly.

When I was cleaning the houses and running Saunders Cleaning Service I still used to get workmen on the site coming up to me and asking for healing. The brickies were forever dropping bricks on their feet and if the wound did not heal they would say, 'Nella, can you help?'

I find myself healing in the most extraordinary places. I will be talking to someone and suddenly I get the feeling that they need help or they will say to me coyly, 'I've got a bad back or a bad knee' and I know what they are really saying is, 'Help me.'

I have healed in restaurants and offices, in taxis and in the street. I remember, once, I was doing a radio show with Brian Matthews and in the middle of the programme he suddenly said, 'You can heal, can you?'

'Yes,' I said.

'Well can you heal my arm?' He had a stiff shoulder, I think.

'When?' I said.

'Now,' he said. So I got up, took off my earphones and healed him while he carried on talking on the radio. It worked too!

I have never turned anyone away but, to be honest, I have wished I did not have the gift. If you have the gift you do not have a life of your own, you cannot say no. To say no, I really believe, would be the most wicked thing in the world. If somebody came to you at midnight and said, 'Help me, I'm in terrible pain,' and you knew you had the gift of healing you couldn't tell them to go away and come back tomorrow, could you?

If some old dear rings me up on the phone and says, 'Nella, I can't stand this anymore, please come round,' I go. There is no question, no debate. It is my job, my duty, my destiny, if you like.

But then there are the cases that really work and somehow, however tired I feel, however much I think, 'Yes, God, but what about me?' these cases make it all worthwhile.

There are the old people who are at last liberated from pain and free to enjoy life, the young people who give you a thankyou smile that lights up their entire face, and the people who become friends. Donald in Derbyshire is one. I first saw him five years ago. He had emphysema and they told him he only had six months to live. Now he is fine and he still calls me every week.

Sometimes, of course, I have to shut off. Sometimes, when I am healing, if I don't 'clear myself' afterwards the pain goes into me. I actually feel the pain that the patient has been feeling. I could take pain away from you and get it in exactly the same part of my body.

Maybe it is something that I am meant to experience occasionally so I can understand more about the suffering of the person I am treating. But, on the whole, I have to safeguard against that otherwise I could not go on and help anyone else.

I have got to cut it off, stop myself, and I do it by mentally bringing down a screen and cutting myself off from the patient. Anyway, what would I gain by all that love flowing back into me? What do you gain if you are full of love and you keep it to yourself? Where is the pleasure in that? Your love, my love, is only meaningful and rewarding when it is given out.

Of course the patient can himself, or herself, help at a healing session. *You* can help me to make it, whatever this gift is, work. That doesn't mean if you go along to a healing session you have to have one hundred per cent faith that it will work. It may not, and no one has ever been angry with me if it hasn't. But it does help the healer if you go along with a very open mind. Try not to go there with any preconceptions. Keep your mind open to the experience and, just as important, keep your heart open too.

If you are not well it is understandably easy to feel anger and bitterness. Why you? Why should you have to go through this suffering? I can't answer that.

All I can say is that if you go to a healing session you will help yourself if you make a conscious effort to cast out negative thoughts. Go along knowing that all the thoughts there are positive. These thoughts are warm, they are thoughts of love and that is really the operative word. Love is the king pin of the universe and, if you can go to a session with love in your mind, you will not lose out. Even if you are not completely cured, you are still going to get something from the experience. You are going to feel better.

Using love, I have even managed mass healing over the radio – although I have only tried it once and would not do it again because it was so draining.

Every month I do a phone-in show on Radio Thamesmead our local radio station here in South London. Steve George is the host of the show and people ring in for clairvoyance and guidance. I speak to them on the phone and I can usually pick something up. They say, 'Hello Nella' and then the feeling comes through to me. I say something like, 'Just a minute, there's a lot of worry around you. It's your daughter you're worried about . . .'

One month, last year, I suddenly thought that I could use the show to do mass healing. To be honest, I wasn't sure if it would work and I was intrigued to see what the effect would be.

Steve agreed to let me try. When I first started on his show he was an adamant non-believer in anything paranormal. When I did my first show I could feel him watching me and, when I looked over at him, I could see he had gone as white as a sheet at what I was saying. Suffice to say, he's no longer a non-believer!

After I had done the clairvoyance over the air, I said to the listeners, 'Now I'm going to try a little experiment. Anyone who needs some medical help or anyone who's not feeling well . . . I want you to stand in front of your radio.'

Then I told them what I was going to do. 'I want you to imagine, as you listen to my voice, that I'm there with you and I'm using my hands to heal you. I'm putting my hands gently on your head, now my hands are slowly moving down your body . . .'

We waited in the studio for the reaction and it was not long before all the phone lines were buzzing. I think some of the listeners had not even wanted healing. They just wanted to stand in front of their radios to see what happened. But they all reported the same effect: they all said they felt a sense of peace and relaxation. A lot of illness is illness we create for ourselves through tension. When you get the fantastic sensation of healing, this lovely feeling, the tension goes and you immediately feel better.

I often wish I could do it to myself but unfortunately I can't. I have tried but it just does not work. Yet I can heal myself of aches and pains and you can, too, if you work at it.

I used to have terrible asthma but I cured myself of that, and last year I had a terrible bout of viral pneumonia. The doctors would not give me anything for it because they were not sure what was wrong with me, but they did discover that the white blood cells in my blood had increased alarmingly.

First of all, I knew I was very weak so I had to get my body strong. That meant rest, and more rest, and, of course, light but nourishing foods.

Then, when I felt my physical strength returning, I lifted my mind by positive thought, by thinking happy things, by being optimistic. I know, when you are feeling rotten, that is easier said than done but it really is the key to healing yourself and, believe me, it works.

You feel miserable, you feel depressed, but you must lift yourself out of that depression. It does not matter much how you do it but you must be very strong with yourself. The very tone of your mind must be lifted.

Put on some happy music, do something that usually gives you pleasure, cast your mind back to happy memories of the past and tell yourself that one day you are going to be happy like that again.

Dream of all the lovely things you want to do in the future, then say to yourself, 'I want to do that and I'm going to do that but I can't do that if I'm feeling like this. So I'm not going to feel like this. I'm going to feel better than this.'

Feel the love inside yourself, not just the love of yourself or the love that other people give to you, but your love of the world, your love of other people. Build yourself up on love.

Then say to yourself, 'OK, I've got this pain in my leg. I don't want this pain in my leg. Go away pain in my leg.'

Say it with conviction and you will be surprised because, before you know where you are, the pain in your leg is easing.

By using your mind and your love, you can ease pain in most

areas of the body, although I do think it is very hard to kill pains in your head. Headaches are the very devil to get rid of. I have got a fairly high pain threshold but I am plagued with headaches every day of my life and I have to take pain killers like everyone else.

But if the pain is in your arm or your back or your knee you can cope with it. You may not be able to cure it but you can, with practice, come to terms with it. The technique is similar to that used by those Indian mystics who walk over hot coals without apparently feeling a twinge of pain. It is mind over matter.

You can accept the pain and go with it. You can say, 'This pain is part of me and I accept it.' Once you have done that you can then say, 'This is a part of me I do not want.' And you can actually make it go away.

Or you can create a diversion away from the pain. This is especially effective if you know you are going to suffer sudden pain; for example if you are going to have some stitches done at the doctor's or you are about to have a nasty filling at the dentist. You focus your mind away from the pain.

Say, for example, you are going to have a big injection in your thigh. Do not think about your thigh. Your thigh does not exist. It is no longer part of you. Instead press together the thumb and forefinger of your right hand as hard as you can. Or, push the thumb of one hand into the centre of the palm of the other as hard as you can.

Now concentrate, really concentrate, on *that* feeling – what your thumb is feeling. You will hardly notice the needle in your thigh at all.

I am a great believer in the power of herbs and plants to heal, and in homeopathy, the theory that you treat like with like but in minuscule quantities. But I am not a homeopathic doctor so don't ask me for homeopathic cures!

But I do believe that in many cases homeopathy can help people and it pleases me to see that more places are offering complementary medicine – there is the physician who treats you with drugs and the alternative doctors who treat you with homeopathy, reflexology, massage, aromatherapy and all that kind of thing. I cannot see why the idea of complementary medicine offends some of those in the field of conventional medicine. It seems like common sense to me.

I have healed with herbs and natural plants, but not directly. Sometimes, when I am healing, the spirit of a beautiful young woman appears at my side. I do not know who she is, or when she walked this earth, but she has a kind of glow about her and I think she must have been a healer many, many years ago.

There is no telling when she will appear and she only comes to me when I am healing certain patients. Then, suddenly, I am aware of her standing at my side and she speaks to me, 'Tell him to make up this recipe or that . . .'

An airline pilot used to come to see me regularly for treatment to his shoulder. I forget exactly what was wrong with him but he visited for several weeks and his complaint was slowly getting better. Then one day, while I was healing him, the woman appeared at my shoulder.

'Ask him about his toe,' she said.

'You've got to take care of your toe, too, my lad,' I said to him.

'What about my toe?'

'You've got a very sore big toe. The nail is split badly.'

'Yes, I have,' he said.

Then, as the woman spoke to me, I passed on her remedy to him. It sounded ridiculous . . .

'When you go home tonight get an ordinary onion, cut it in half and, with the wet side, rub all around your bad toe. Do that every night for three nights. You might stink the place out but it doesn't matter. Do it.'

Next time I heard from him he told me the toe had completely healed after the third night.

The woman healer also appeared to me when I was treating a woman with multiple sclerosis. There was little I could do to halt the progression of the disease but I was easing her discomfort and pain with some success, except for her legs. She had great discomfort in her legs.

The spirit healer told me what to instruct my patient to do.

She was to get fresh, and she emphasised *fresh*, cabbage leaves and to bandage her feet in these cabbage leaves every night, then take them off in the morning. I passed on the remedy and the woman I was healing reported that it worked very well, she felt much better.

My spirit healer also helped me to treat a child with eczema but it was quite a complicated remedy and I do not want to describe it here because, for a start, it may only have been effective with that particular child and, secondly, it is very important that the herbs and plants are prepared properly and I am not sure people would know how to do that. I would hate something to go wrong.

Some of the remedies the woman has given me have been purely cosmetic. She talked to me once about a cure for baldness in men which was very interesting. Unfortunately I can't patent it and make my fortune because it also involves using my healing hands and I do not believe I should use my healing gift merely for cosmetic purposes.

I am always pleased to see my woman healer. She is a beautiful creature and she must have done wonders in her own time, which I can only guess at, but imagine to be a good two hundred years ago.

I do not know anything else about her. She never talks about herself and she never appears to want to use me as a medium to get in touch with anyone in particular on this side. She just appears when she is needed and disappears as soon as I have passed on her remedies. Perhaps she appears to other healers as well. There is no reason to suppose she wouldn't. It would be interesting to find out and compare notes!

I am also a great believer in the power of water to heal. Everyone should drink lots of water every day and, if you are feeling ill, drinking a pint of cold water will invariably make you feel better. As you drink it tell yourself, 'This water is going to heal me, this water is going to make me feel better, this water is going to cleanse me,' and it will. The water will flush out the illness; you are putting in a good liquid to flush out the bad.

Looking at water is wonderful when you are feeling depressed. It does not really matter if it is the water in a fish tank, the water of the sea, a river or a lake, although I think watching moving water is best. Water is free. Watch it and it frees your mind. Imagine you are taking your depression and putting it in the water and it is being carried away. That may sound very silly but it honestly works.

Or, imagine that depression as a big grey cloud that is floating away. In fact, that is just what depression looks like.

I do not actually work very much with auras but everyone has got one. I see them around everyone I meet. Auras come in all shapes, sizes and colours. Some people have a very wide aura, it shines out for about six inches all around them. Other people have narrow auras, maybe just half an inch or even less.

I am very conscious of auras when I am healing. A healthy person's aura is beautiful, like a rainbow, with lots of bright clear colours, oranges, blues and greens. If someone is ill you see very dark colours, the aura is grey and sometimes patchy black. If someone is very ill indeed the aura is all black. Depression turns your aura grey.

If you go to a New Age festival – the kind of fair where they have lots of clairvoyants and tarot readers and sell all kinds of 'psychic' paraphernalia – you will usually find someone who measures auras from the hands. It's called Kirlian photography and all you have to do is put your hand on a plate and a special camera takes a photograph of your palm. From the print you can see the aura all around.

Last time I went to the famous Festival of Mind and Body in London I had mine done just for fun. The aura around my hands was over a foot long, so long it went off the page! You should have seen the photographer's face! Then I explained I was a healer . . .

I have healing hands, but so do you. You instinctively use them to heal, even though you do not realise you are doing it. If you knock yourself you automatically rub it better, and you use your love.

Imagine a mother and child. The child falls over and hurts its knee. Mother says, 'Oh, I'll kiss it better,' and she does and it *is* better because there is an unseen love link going from the mother to the child.

And you have that love inside you too. If someone is ill or upset, you put out your hands and touch them, you put out your hands to help, to comfort, and, instinctively, to heal. There is no mystery to it. It is simply love. Healing is really the most natural thing in the world.

FOUR

Lost Souls

'Our four-year-old grandson, Simon, had been missing for weeks before I said I wanted to call in a psychic. Our family were desperate. The police had been wonderful, they were searching everywhere and working very hard. But I thought we should do all that we could.

'I had never met a psychic before and I didn't quite know what to expect. I was a bit surprised that Nella was an ordinary person just like us! She was very nice. She came up to visit us three times and searching with her really helped me. It made me feel we were actually doing something rather than just sitting at home waiting for news.

'Other people had suggested that Simon had been taken miles away, but all along Nella said he was still nearby, somewhere local. She drew an area with a one-mile radius and the place where Simon was eventually found was right in the middle of that area.

'We took Nella to Hemel old town and she said, "Simon is near here." He was. She also said that he was within earshot of church bells – he was found 100 yards from a church.

'Simon was found alive and well and he's doing fine now. We were very, very lucky. It was a terrible time and Nella helped us a lot. It was a great comfort to have her here. She's a lovely lady. It's difficult to understand but I do believe she has a special gift.'

MRS JEAN STEVENS,
Grandmother of Simon Jones who was abducted
from his home in Hemel Hempstead in 1990.

'I was sceptical when we went to see Nella but at the time we were groping about in the dark and we were willing to try anything. Now I am not so sceptical.

'There was no hocus pocus, no darkened room or crystal ball. She was a very pleasant, friendly and ordinary lady. She gave us tea and cakes and then she started to talk.

'I have to say that much of what she said was very general and could have fitted many circumstances. But then, while she was out of the room, I laid a selection of photos of people and places on the floor and as soon as she came back in she immediately pointed out two men. These pictures had never been published so there was no way she could have known who the people were.

'One of those men was in the dock accused of Julie's murder although he has, in fact, now been cleared.

'Nella also reacted strongly to a picture of an old toilet block with a corrugated roof. "Why did they hold her there?" she said. The police had not searched the block but after talking to Nella I returned to Kenya and searched it myself. In a cubicle I found one of Julie's hairs.

'That evidence was a great help. I have never been involved with psychics before or since but I have to say I think Nella is a remarkable lady.'

JOHN WARD,
Father of Julie Ward who went missing in Kenya

Earlier this year I got a phone call from a woman who sounded absolutely desperate. She said her daughter and grandchild had gone missing in America after a fight with her son-in-law and she was convinced that something terrible had happened.

'I know she's dead,' she said. 'I know it.'

I immediately knew the girl was not dead.

'No, she isn't,' I told the woman. 'She isn't dead.'

'But we're so close,' said her mother. 'She would have contacted me, I know she would.'

'She's not dead and she will contact you very soon.'

A week later the girl phoned to say she and the child were fine, but the mother still does not know exactly where, in America, her daughter is, for the simple reason that she does not want anyone to know where she is – and that includes Mum whether Mum likes it or not.

That story illustrates perfectly why I do not enjoy getting involved in missing persons cases. Yes, I could probably have found the girl, but I have to respect people's wishes. If someone is adult they have the right to privacy and, sometimes, that means the right to escape alone.

Who am I to barge in and say, 'Well, I know where you are?'

I have done that before and I have regretted it. A couple of years ago I got a call from Maurice Rowitz, a handsome, young private investigator who works in the North of England. He called and offered me a job.

'Nella,' he said. 'I want you to find a body.' And he told me the man's names.

'Are you sure he's dead?' I said.

'No question,' said Maurice. 'The police are convinced he's dead. He hasn't been seen for months. He hasn't drawn his social security benefit and he is slightly mentally backward.'

I smiled. 'This man is not dead,' I said.

'You're wrong,' said Maurice, 'and his parents are desperate to find his body. Will you come up?'

The answer, as always, was yes and I took the train to Nottingham where Maurice met me at the station.

'Where do you want to go first?'

'The local psychiatric hospital,' I said.

I knew I had to go there. I concentrated on the photo of the missing man and I just knew. It was the same feeling that had swept over me all those years ago when Eric and I sought out my father so we could get permission to marry.

When we got to the hospital it was a grim place. In the foyer three men were talking among themselves. As I looked at them, I suddenly had a picture in my mind of the missing man standing next to one of the three men. He had on a long overcoat in a sort of herringbone pattern and I was sure he had worn the same coat when he was with the man we were looking for.

I went up to him, tapped him on the shoulder and showed him the photograph.

'Excuse me, have you seen this man recently?'

If he thought it was a funny request he didn't let on. He just said, 'Yes, that's my friend.'

'When did you last see him?'

'About three weeks ago.'

'So he's alive and well, then?'

'Of course.'

That was the first contact.

Next, I had the feeling I wanted to go to Nottingham town centre. When we arrived I led Maurice down a slope into a kind of piazza and I felt drawn to a young girl pavement artist who was busy drawing a colourful landscape on one of the slabs. I showed her the photograph.

'When did you last see this man, sweetheart?'

'About ten minutes ago,' she said. 'He wore a little cross as an earring. It came out and he asked me to help him put it back in.'

Maurice and I walked on a little farther until my feet took me to an Italian cafe. We went in and again I showed the photograph.

'Oh, he's always around here,' said the owner. 'He stands outside looking through the window, but he doesn't come in.'

Maurice, by this time, had fallen into a stunned silence. It was only an hour or so since I had got off the Inter City train. The question he wanted to ask was, 'How did I know?' But I could not answer that. It was just as if invisible hands were leading me on and my psychic eye was showing me the people I had to talk to.

Next, I was led on through the town centre to a pub. Outside there was a young man with very blonde hair and I knew, before I even spoke to him, that he had a speech impediment.

I showed him the photograph and he said, 'Oh, are you the people he was waiting for? Because he was waiting here just a minute ago.'

'Where did he go?'

'To the bus station.'

So we went to the bus station but we had just missed him.

I knew he was on a bus heading South so we went to see the boy's parents to reassure them that he was alive and well. But they would have none of it. They still swore that he was dead.

The next day the story appeared in the local papers in Nottingham. All the time I had the feeling there was more to this case than people thought and I also knew within me that the man had seen the papers and was travelling towards London because he wanted to see me. He wanted someone to talk to.

But he never made it. Inevitably, his family found him and when they got him back they had him sectioned and put into the psychiatric hospital indefinitely. I think that was wrong and when I heard what had happened I thought, 'I wish to God I'd never told them where he was. It was cruel.' To this day I am convinced that he was not mentally ill, the poor man. He was just 'different', and all of us have a right to be different.

So, you can see, getting involved in missing persons cases isn't always straightforward. Does the person want to be found? Should they be found? What right do I have to tell other people where they are?

The most famous case that brought home to me this dilemma was the case of missing earl Lord Lucan who disappeared after the family nanny, Sandra Rivett, was found murdered in the Lucans' Belgravia home in November, 1974.

The alarm was raised later one Thursday evening when Lord Lucan's wife ran from her house shouting, 'Murder!' Covered in blood, she stumbled into a nearby pub and screamed, 'I am dying and my nanny has been killed!'

A warrant was issued for the earl's arrest and one police theory at the time was that it was a case of mistaken identity. Lady Lucan and Sandra Rivett, who had started her job there only five weeks earlier, were of a similar age and build.

In the dim light of the basement room where she was murdered the earl could have struck at the wrong woman.

Like everyone else I read the story in the newspapers, then, one morning, the telephone rang and it was Chelsea CID. They were looking for Lucan but he seemed to have vanished into thin air. All kinds of theories were being bandied about: he had killed himself, he had driven off a cliff, he had caught a cross-channel ferry to France, he had flown off in a friend's private plane.

I do not enjoy getting involved with the police on cases of missing persons. For a start, they have usually got several psychics working on the case anyway. The family are searching, the police are searching and it is extremely difficult not to pick up their thoughts instead of being able to home in on the person who has actually disappeared.

But, I admit, the Lucan case intrigued me so I told the police on the case I would consider working on it. After I had talked to one policeman I was convinced we had to go to a place near Milton Keynes, the new town north of London.

Three officers picked me up in their unmarked car and we drove off up the A1. I knew where we were going. I mean, I had never been there in my life before, but I could see it in my mind just as if it was a film on my television.

I said, 'There's a house called Ivy Grange. Behind the house there's a canal and moored just by the house is a blue and white boat. But, before then, we come to a plough without a horse.'

We arrived in a village and there in front of us was a pub called *The Plough* – it had a big sign outside, just a plough with no horse. Then one of the policemen asked a passing local if there was a place anywhere around the village called Ivy Grange. It was no problem. You needed to go straight up the road, turn this way and that, and there was a big house called Ivy Grange. As we approached the house we went over a bridge and there, behind the house, was the canal and a blue and white boat tied up at the water's edge at the end of the garden.

We parked outside the house and one of the officers went in to investigate. He was gone for a long time but when he came out he was grinning all over his face.

He looked at his colleague.

'That's where he's been hiding out,' he said. Then we drove back to town.

'Had Lucan been in the house?' I asked.

'Oh no,' they said and that was as much as I could get out of them. But later I found out why they were so pleased.

Before the Lucan case they had been working on another case entirely and, for a long time, they had been searching for a certain criminal they thought was responsible. As it turned out, I had led them to the house where he had been hiding.

In my thoughts I had gone back in time but, instead of picking up Lucan, I had picked up the case the policemen were working on earlier. Which just goes to show how wrong you can be!

That is where my involvement with the police ended. But it was not the end of the Lucan case, as far as I was concerned. About a week later the phone rang and a man said, 'Nella, this friend of ours has gone missing and we're very worried about him. We don't know where he is, even if he's alive or dead. Can you help?'

The man and his friend came down to my house and we all sat in the sitting room.

'We thought this might help,' they said and gave me a scrap of paper with some handwriting on it. I held it and I kept saying, 'Lucky, lucky. I don't know why I keep getting that word but this man is very lucky.'

The two men looked at each other. Then, as I was holding the piece of paper, I suddenly saw Lord Lucan's face in front of me. I was livid. I do not like being cheated by anyone. I threw the piece of paper back at them.

'This isn't a friend of yours,' I said. 'You're not looking for a friend, you're looking for Lord Lucan!'

Then they admitted they were reporters from the *News of the World*!

In fact, I had already picked up quite a lot about Lucky Lucan and what had happened that night. Every now and then, pictures of him would flash through my mind. I still believe he is innocent. He did not kill Sandra Rivett. I told the detectives that he had a pilot's licence and was quite capable of flying himself out of the country.

They said, 'We didn't know about that.'

So I said, 'Well you'd better check up on it.'

They did, and I was right.

I told the reporters that he had a very strange scar at the back of one of his ears. Afterwards they talked to his wife, Lady Lucan, and I was right. But she was upset and kept asking them, 'How does this woman know this about my husband?'

I know there was great confusion that night, terrible confusion. In the pictures I was 'seeing', Lord Lucan was walking past the house, then he walked back and went in. Sandra Rivett was already dead, Lucan arrived just as the murderer was making his escape out of the back of the house.

It was almost as if Lucan was 'set up' for the job, but he did not commit the crime. All those stories about Sandra being killed because she was mistaken for Lady Lucan were absolute rubbish, as far as I am concerned. Every person has their own presence. If you were in a darkened room with your husband, you would know it was your husband. If you were in a darkened room with a stranger, you would know it was a stranger.

We all have our own scent, our own way of moving, our own aura. Also, there was a certain amount of light in the room and Sandra cried out. Lucan would have known, then, that it was not his wife.

Lucan left and he went to see friends in Sussex but then he took a very strange route. He doubled back on himself, again and again. He did not go straight to his destination. He left the country by air and he had a lot of help on the way, I can tell you that for sure.

He ended up in Nairobi and he lived there for quite a long time. Then he moved to the South of France and, now, he has moved on elsewhere. He is still very much alive and he looks just like his pictures, only considerably older of course. He has visited Britain several times but he has never been even close to being caught and I am pleased about that.

I could find him now, but I have made a vow I am not going to tell anyone where he is for the simple reason that the man is innocent and he has no hope of proving that at the moment.

I do not regard finding missing people as my main job. My job, my life's work, is healing and clairvoyance. Searching for missing people is a distraction from that, and I need all my energy for my true vocation.

It is a very different field altogether and when I work on missing persons cases I feel totally different. There is always an air of desperation around the people who are searching and it is infectious. Quite often a man or woman will turn up on my doorstep and ask me to help them to find a wife, a husband, or a lover who has left them. I try to say no. You do not know what state the marriage was in beforehand. There are things they try to cover up which, if I want to, I can uncover, but I do not want to uncover all the dirt in someone's private life. That is nothing to do with me, that is their personal problem. I do not want to do that. That is not what I am here for.

Cases of missing children are undoubtedly the worst. You cannot help being emotionally involved. Everyone is, the police as well as the family, and everyone is so desperate for me to find the child the pressure makes it hard to concentrate. But, the relief when the case has a happy ending and the child is found alive, is overwhelming.

I was called in by a newspaper in 1990 when Simon Jones, a little boy from Hemel Hempstead in Hertfordshire, went missing. He was only four years old and, understandably, his family were frantic. As I walked around his village, I was terribly afraid that he was dead.

I believed that he might be dead because I could not see him moving about. When I am looking for someone, I see moving pictures in my mind. I see the person moving around and I see the surroundings they are in. Sometimes, the place is very clear, as if it was on video, but the edges, the outside of the picture, is all furry.

I often see signs – a bridge, a house, a strange shaped tree, a name. These are psychic clues, but I still cannot see exactly where they are. All I can do is trust my instinct to lead me to the clues and I know I will recognise them when I get there.

Sometimes, driving around with the police, looking for the psychic clues in my head, I feel I am going to go crazy. It is so frustrating.

I could not see Simon moving around and I could not see his surroundings. Everything was dark but I did say all along that the man who had abducted him was a local man. I kept getting the word, 'Bell, bell, bell.' I thought that, wherever he was, if he was still alive, he could hear bells.

I drew a triangle on a map. I knew that, alive or dead, Simon was somewhere within that triangle. The area was close to Simon's home and, with the newspaper reporter, we tramped over the fields within that triangle while I looked for psychic clues. I could see in my mind's pictures an old mill and, nearby, a disused railway line. We found both but, although I talked to people in both places, we seemed no nearer to finding the little boy. I could see in my mind a little tunnel and I could smell the man who abducted him. He smelt absolutely foul.

I passed on all that I had managed to pick up to the police, but I went home feeling depressed that I had not been able to help more. That night I prayed for Simon's safe return.

Thank God, a couple of weeks later he was found, shaken but alive and well, in a men's hostel not far from his home. Afterwards John Higgs, the police superintendent in charge of the case, rang me. The house in which they had found Simon was opposite a church called St. Margaret's where, every Sunday, they rang the bells – and on the corner of this road was a pub called The Bell. Where Simon was being held, the man had built a kind of tunnel through which the little boy had to crawl to get to the bathroom so no one else in the house would see he was there.

And, finally, John told me, 'You were right about the smell, Nella. The man stank to high heaven.'

So, you can see how the clues turn out right in the end. It is how you interpret them along the way that counts. If you interpret them correctly you are led to the right place.

The Simon Jones case reminded me of a case I worked on in 1978: the search for Devon schoolgirl Genette Tate. Then, too, I picked up a wealth of clues which seemed to lead me round and round in circles in an apparently meaningless pattern.

Sadly, the story of Genette did not have a happy ending.

Genette was a pretty thirteen-year-old when she disappeared. It was a baffling case. No one could quite understand it. On a hot summer's afternoon she had been doing a paper round in the village of Aylesbeare, standing in, just for that day, for a school friend.

Then she vanished. Her bicycle, and the newspapers she had been carrying, were found abandoned in a country lane but, despite hundreds of hours of police investigation, enormous publicity and massive search-parties combing the area, there was no sign of her.

I knew Genette was dead as soon as I read of her disappearance and I travelled many times to Devon in the search for Genette's body. With police and reporters, I drove for what seemed like hours through the beautiful green lanes of the Devon countryside.

Time and again, I knew my psychic clues were leading me in the right direction. Without being told I managed to pinpoint on a map the exact place where Genette's bicycle had been found. From there I traced her route – the same route, I later discovered, that many other psychics on the case, including the famous Dutch psychic Gerard Crioset, had plotted.

I kept getting the name of the village of Kilmington and, on one visit, we drove in that direction. I told the reporter with me that we would come to a broken road sign, then a bridge. I saw a white house fronted by clusters of bright flowers; I saw a river winding through the fields and I told them that, when we reached the right spot, we would see five tree stumps and two big white birds flying above. They would circle three times above us and then fly off.

One by one my clues became reality: the broken sign, the bridge, the white house, the field and the river and, as we arrived at the field I had seen in my mind's eye, we saw the tree stumps and two swans above us. They circled three times and disappeared.

In the field I was looking for a drain which, I was sure, was important. It took some time but, eventually, we discovered a cesspit surrounded by concrete and covered by heavy wooden railway sleepers. The following day the police searched the cesspit but without success. Nothing! I could hardly believe it and I went home with a heavy heart. I knew I had been on the right track, I knew it. I had missed something, I must have done.

Back home in Bexleyheath I could not forget Genette. I felt she was with me day and night and one evening I heard a voice saying to me, 'Look. You didn't look.'

I am still sure that if I had stayed longer in Devon I would have found her. Two years ago police hoped the mystery was solved when someone came forward claiming to know what had happened to Genette. The person said Genette had been accidently knocked over and killed by a motorist and the panic-stricken driver had buried her in a secret grave. But, after investigations, the story was dismissed by detectives as a cruel hoax.

My heart goes out to her mother. It is awful for a family not to know, to have those lingering doubts and hopes. It is only human to hope, you cannot help it even when hope is, logically, totally unfounded.

Usually, if someone comes to see me about a missing loved one, I know immediately whether they are dead or alive. Last year a group of young people from London came to see me. They had all been on a mountaineering holiday in Switzerland and one day one of their friends, a young man, had disappeared. He seemed to have vanished off the face of the earth.

The local police had searched everywhere but could not find him. Of course, they were all terribly upset. I knew immediately and one young woman looked at me.

'You think he's dead Nella, don't you?' she said.

I didn't know what to say. In the end, all I could say was, 'I don't want to lie to you, but I have to say I can't see him alive.'

After a fortnight he was found dead in a crevasse.

I can rarely bring myself to say to a person in despair, 'I'm sorry, he's dead.' It's too cruel. And who am I to tell? Anyway, I could be wrong. Just because I cannot see the person moving around does not necessarily mean they are dead – look at the case of Simon Jones. But, unfortunately, if I feel someone is dead, I am usually right.

Only last year my local police rang and asked me to help them find a man called Brian Potts. His wife, Christine, turned out to be a lovely lady and she was in a terrible state. She was convinced that he was alive, somewhere up on Dartford Heath. Maybe he had been in an accident, she said, and was lying there, needing help.

So, on Good Friday, a search party was organised. There was a policeman and dozens of local people and we all went up on the Heath and searched. I went too. But as we were walking across the heathland I said to the policeman next to me, 'He's not here, you know.'

'Where do you think he is, Nella?'

I pointed over to the East.

'He's over there, he's lying in a pit and he's dead.'

I knew it was a waste of time searching for him on the Heath but it was something we had to do. For Christine's benefit. She needed to search, she needed that physical experience of searching.

Christine kept looking at me and as I looked back into her eyes I could see she was not ready for the truth yet. I had to keep what I knew to myself for a while longer at least. So I said to Christine, 'We'll keep searching.'

A couple of weeks later she phoned me and I knew I had to tell her.

'I've got some posters printed,' she said. 'I'm going to put them all around the area.'

'Take them down to Gravesend, love,' I said.

'Why Gravesend?'

'Because, Christine, I believe your husband is dead and he's lying in a pit in that area.'

Two days later that is where they found him. I was worried about Christine, I was not sure how she would cope but, thank God, she said to me, 'If you'd told me about Brian earlier I couldn't have taken it. I think I can come to terms with it now.'

I felt very sad for her and it is sad for me too. It is not a good feeling when you know that someone is lying dead, when you can see them. I cannot say it is a creepy feeling, or a shivery feeling – it's not. But it is depressing.

Sometimes, in fact quite often, I am asked to find one person and I end up finding another. Or, I am working on one case and I stumble on a bigger crime. That happened to me when a newspaper called me in to help find baby Alexandra Griffiths who had been stolen from London's St Thomas's Hospital in the winter of 1990.

Baby Alexandra was just 36 hours old when she was snatched from her hospital cot by a woman, desperate for a baby of her own, who posed as a social worker.

For the next 17 days the police mounted a massive search for Alexandra while the 35-year-old woman showed off her 'new baby' in the sleepy Cotswold market town of Burford where she was living.

It was only after a local estate agent became suspicious and phoned the police that Alexandra was rescued. The woman, Janet Griffiths, was committed to hospital for obviously much-needed treatment. She later confessed she had tried to con the boyfriend she was in love with that the baby was his. She was released last year.

I always thought the case an odd one. The woman was supposed to have taken the baby, walked out of the hospital and driven north to her new home. That does not tie in with the visions I had at the time. I could see a car, some kind of service car, waiting.

I saw the woman taking the baby and walking through the hospital with the little mite in her arms and I told the newspaper that I could see her passing a doctor on the stairs on the way out. That was later confirmed by the police.

But I saw her driving south in the first instance and then doubling back towards the north. I was very surprised, too, when I read that only one person had been involved in the kidnap. I saw two people involved. This time, maybe, my visions were wrong as the police have found nothing to back my suspicions. I suppose I will never know.

It was while I was concentrating on Alexandra that babies kept coming into my mind. Not one, but hundreds of them and I kept getting the place names: France and Belgium. At first, since Alexandra was still missing, I thought this might be where she had been taken.

But, gradually, the picture changed. Alexandra was not there but plenty of other babies were. It was a big house, it looked like an old manor house, school or hospital and it was full of babies. And I could see a man and a woman and the man was writing a cheque for £40,000.

I am convinced that there is a world-wide baby stealing racket in operation. I think there is an organisation which is responsible for stealing babies from many different continents – including America and Europe. The babies are then taken to this house in France or Belgium – I know that the staff there speak French – and then, they are sold to childless couples for vast sums of money. Occasionally, I get flashes of pictures of this place. I have not yet, consciously, concentrated on locating the house but I know it will come to me eventually.

When I am working on cases involving children I make a deliberate effort not to get too involved. You do get involved, of course. But you have to protect yourself otherwise you would go out of your mind. You have got to know when enough is enough, then switch off.

At that point I try to think about ordinary things like, 'What are we going to have for supper?' and, 'Did I do the ironing?' I have to come back to mundane things, everyday life. You can switch on the power in the same way. You push the everyday worries completely out of your mind and concentrate solely, and hard, on the person you are looking for.

A lot of people joke that, because of my gift, I could keep a check on all my family and friends if I wanted to! In fact, it is much harder with people I know. Besides, for me to find out what my family and friends are up to just out of idle curiosity would achieve nothing. I treat the gift I have with great respect and I do not go wasting it on silly games that can't achieve anything.

Looking through my psychic eye for the bodies of murder victims is, as you can well imagine, traumatic. You can pick up all the anguish of the person who is searching and often you can also pick up all the suffering and pain of the person who has been killed.

Mr John Ward, a 58-year-old hotelier from Bury St Edmunds in Suffolk, had already found the body of his daughter Julie when he rang me in November, 1990.

'You have probably heard of my case,' he said. 'It's my daughter, Julie, who was murdered in Kenya.'

'How can I help you?'

'I want to find the man who killed her. May I come and see you?'

I was glad to see him. The circumstances of Julie's death were horrific and anything I could do to help I would. The story briefly was this . . .

Julie was twenty-eight years old when she died. After a happy childhood, she had worked for typesetting companies for a number of years before setting off on the adventure of a lifetime – an overland trek of Africa.

She had been travelling for seven months when, in September 1988, her parents were told that she had disappeared in the Masai Mara game reserve in Kenya.

As soon as Mr Ward heard of his daughter's disappearance he flew to Nairobi to look for Julie himself. Later, according to *The Times*, a court heard that, on his arrival, Mr Ward found that 'no proper search was under way and that the police had been informed but nothing was being done.'

Mr Ward knew that Julie had been driving a Suzuki jeep and he knew the location of her last campsite. He chartered six light aircraft to search for her because he believed, or maybe hoped, that she had been in a car accident on the way back from the game reserve to Nairobi.

On the second day of the search they discovered Julie's Suzuki. Some distance away, farther up the road, poor Mr Ward found his daughter's remains on the ashes of a fire in the bush.

Later he said, 'I found my daughter's left leg, or the bottom half of it, some 15 feet from the fire. I found the two halves of my daughter's jaw bone probably another 10 feet away, a lock of hair by the side of the fire, and within the ashes, several other items including pieces of bone.'

There were stories being told at the time in Kenya, that Julie had been eaten by wild animals. John Ward thought his daughter had been murdered and he set out to prove it and to find her killer.

He would not give up. Two years later he arrived at my house with his wife and a pile of photographs, all different, but all of African men. He wanted me to go through the pictures one by one in the hope that I might pick up something from one of them.

And I did. What I did not tell him and his wife, what I could not tell them, was that all the time I was also seeing pictures of Julie's last days flashing through my mind. It was horrific. Those men are no more than animals. But, I could not tell the Wards what I saw. They were distressed enough already.

I looked through the photos. I wasn't really looking at the faces, as such, and I immediately felt drawn to one of the men. This was a wicked man.

I gave the photograph to Mr Ward. 'That is the man who murdered your daughter,' I said. Then I looked through some more pictures. I came to the photo of another man. He was involved too.

'And this man, he was involved somehow too. He may have helped the other man. He may have been there. He knows what happened. He is guilty too.'

Pictures kept flashing through my mind. Julie. Her car had broken down. She walked away, looking for help. The men said they would help her but they didn't . . . I could see a big lorry, a truck, a man delivering goods . . .

'There is a man with a lorry, he's involved too,' I told them. 'I'm not sure how. But he knows all about it.'

Mr and Mrs Ward took away the photographs with the two I had picked out and I wished them luck. I hoped I had helped them. There was one piece of good news I could tell them.

'The men responsible for your daughter's murder will be brought to trial and they will be convicted.'

As I am writing this, more than four years after Julie's death, in the early months of 1992, there is an extraordinary trial taking place in a courtroom in Nairobi. Two former rangers from the Makari ranger station – Jonah Nagiroi, aged 28 and Peter Kipeen, aged 27 – stand in the dock denying Julie's murder.

I do not know if these are the men whose photos I picked out of that pile, and I would not say for one minute that my meeting with John Ward has had any influence on the proceedings. As the British newspapers have reported, what Mr Ward has presented to the court have been hard facts, evidence which he himself, with great determination, has uncovered. *The Daily Telegraph* wrote earlier this year:

'For more than three years Mr Ward has been engaged in a remorseless quest to find the killers of Miss Ward . . . He launched the first real search . . . was there when her remains were found, collected statements and scientific evidence, commissioned the only genuine post-mortem examination and has been a thorn in the side of Kenyan officials who wanted to keep the case under wraps.

'This has been his investigation, and without his courage and tenacity the murder charges would not have been brought . . .'

To all of that I say, 'Hear, hear.'

After the Wards left I felt very drained and desperately sad for them. As I was sitting in my armchair thinking about the case Julie came to me. I did not see her in spirit but I immediately sensed she was there and she was talking to me. She was telling me little personal details, not to do with the murder but connected with her life at home. She asked me to contact her mother, to reassure her that she was now at peace and I did as she asked. I telephoned Mrs Ward that evening and passed on to her everything Julie had told me.

These were details of family life I could not possibly have known about but, as I talked to Mrs Ward, she kept saying, 'Yes, that's right. Yes, that's right.'

I think what I told her comforted her. At least, I very much hope it did.

I have great admiration for that couple and, in my opinion, Mr Ward is a fantastic man. When they heard the terrible news of Julie's disappearance they were not prepared to merely sit there and take it – they wanted to do something about it. They wanted to find the truth. On a basic level, the circumstances were suspicious, but I think it was more than that. I believe that had an in-born sense, a psychic sense, that they had been told lies.

I have heard since that some people believe that Mr Ward's cru-
sade to get at the facts of his daughter's death, his determination to
find the truth, may have made life even worse for the family. Wouldn't
it have been better to let matters lie before he endangered his own life
through the stress and strain of it all?

I cannot agree with that. It is the truth that sets you free. It is not
a matter of revenge, it is a matter of justice. I think he was right not to
rest until he caught the alleged culprits and saw them standing in the
dock. Not knowing is worse. However painful the truth is, it is only
when we have the truth that we can accept it, maybe grieve because of
it, but then be able to move on to live the rest of our lives fully. Once
the Wards see that justice has been done, I hope they can go forward
and enjoy their life together in peace and happiness before they are
reunited with Julie.

Sometimes, people come to me with the most extraordinary
requests and, of course, I can use my gift to find anyone or anything –
not only people. One of my most interesting missing persons cases was
not to do with a missing person at all, but with a missing horse!

They called Shergar a 'wonder horse'. He had won both the
English and Irish Derbies – the English Derby by a record ten lengths
in 1981. He was worth £10 million to his owner, the Aga Khan, and,
more than that, he had not only class but charisma.

It was hardly surprising, then, that every racegoer in the country
was devastated when he was snatched from the Aga Khan's Irish stud
farm in County Kildare, Ireland, in the cold February of 1983.

What happened to him after that remains a mystery – well, to
most people, but not to me. The kidnappers demanded a ransom of
£2,000,000. There were stories that he had been kidnapped by the
IRA who then killed him after the Aga Khan refused to pay the money.
But even last year, in 1991, there were stories in the newspapers that
Shergar was, in fact, alive and well and grazing in the Channel Islands.

Insurers, Lloyd's, had paid out £3,620,000 to Shergar's owners
so they were understandably shocked when they were contacted by a
group of bounty hunters who claimed Shergar was alive – and were
seeking a reward for their information.

A man from Lloyd's confirmed that he had been contacted but
added, 'We have no concrete proof and I am very sceptical.'

He was right to be so. Horse-lovers on the Channel Island of
Guernsey, where Shergar was supposed to be enjoying a happy retire-
ment, also described the story as nonsense. I agree with them. Sadly,
Shergar is dead, I am sure of that.

Shergar had been missing for three weeks before a newspaper
called and asked me to help trace him. I knew immediately he was still
in Ireland. I tuned into him just as I would into any missing creature,
human or animal, and, as I did so, I felt he was in a bad state.

The name of Dunkellin, a small hamlet in County Galway, came
to me straight away and the reporters were amazed. There was such a

village on the West Coast of Ireland but it was so small it did not appear on most maps and, as I have never been to Ireland in my life, there is no way I could have heard of the place.

I could see Shergar being held in a single-storey warehouse or shed a few hundred yards from the sea. I could see a pole outside the shed, or nearby, with some kind of triangle secured to the mast and I had the feeling that there was a private airfield nearby. I could see a little church, painted in a light colour, and I was sure that Shergar could hear its bells ringing.

The reporters probably thought that detail a little mad but, when I tune into someone who is missing, I do not only see their surroundings. I hear what they hear, smell what they smell.

As a kidnapping, it was a botched job. I do not know whether the kidnappers were members of the IRA but I doubt it, because these men – and there were at least four of them – were amateurs. They were heavily involved in the racing scene but, when it came to actually looking after a horse as opposed to merely betting on one, they did not have a clue.

The motive for the kidnapping was, of course, money. But the kidnappers were interested in more than the ransom money. They had a plan that, before they received the money and returned the horse, they would mate Shergar with mares of their own. In that way they could sell the foals for vast sums of money – and they would have numerous 'certs' running around the racetracks of Britain and Ireland for years to come.

I could actually 'see' two mares being brought to Shergar in a white-painted van.

At first the kidnapping went well. They led Shergar into a van and transported him to the hamlet on the West Coast. But then they started to argue among themselves and, with so much publicity, they began to get scared.

These men were petty criminals and they just could not take the pressure. Also, they had no idea how to look after a horse of such quality properly. They fed him the wrong foods and very quickly, very soon after they had snatched him, I believe that Shergar fell ill.

Those hunting for Shergar were getting nearer. The net was closing. The kidnappers were worried that they were going to be discovered and, I am sure, Shergar was spotted by someone. Whether this man reported what he saw to the police I do not know. But, to the kidnappers, it was the final straw.

They panicked. Shergar was already in a weak state so they had him put down.

At the time, I told the newspaper that I could feel that Shergar was very weak. A couple of weeks later, I was at home and suddenly I knew with a certainty that he was dead. It was horrible. I saw what they had done. After they had killed him they did not even bury him decently. He was chopped up into pieces and they took him, in a boat out into the rough Atlantic and there they threw the pieces overboard so he would never be discovered.

The men have never been caught but, I am sure, the Irish police, and probably the British police too, know who they are. But no horse – no proof.

One other thing I am sure of. The kidnappers did manage to mate Shergar. In fact, there are far more sons and daughters of Shergar running around the world's racing tracks than people imagine. I am not interested in horse racing so I do not know who wins what, or which horse is which, but I do know that some of Shergar's offspring have done very well indeed. And somebody, somewhere, has made a lot of money.

Sometimes, I use my gift to find objects as well as people and horses! Last year I was introduced by a mutual friend to Miranda Rothschild, a member of the famous Rothschild banking family. Miranda's mother had died and while the family were sorting out her possessions they discovered that a Picasso, which had been in her mother's bedroom, had disappeared. Could I help?

Miranda took me to the house, a beautiful place in London, and I stood in her mother's bedroom. None of the family could remember much about the picture. They knew it was small and defiinitely Picasso, but that was about all because it had been hanging there for so long they took its existence for granted and rarely looked at it properly.

As I stood in the room I felt immediately that the picture was not there. It definitely was not in that room and Miranda confirmed that. It was the first place they had looked; in drawers, in cupboards, even under the bed. As I concentrated I kept getting 'Rubbish tip, rubbish tip.' I told Miranda that it probably sounded silly but I was sure the picture was lying on a rubbish tip somewhere. I could not say exactly where, the picture was very foggy around the edges, but it was not too far away.

I liked Miranda from the first moment I met her so I was disappointed when I could not tell her more.

'Well,' she said, 'You did your best Nella. That's all you can do.'

But I was able to tell her that I thought she would get the picture back – and soon.

That night I was lying in bed listening to LBC, a London radio station, when the ten o'clock news came on the air. I nearly jumped out of bed!

They said a small Picasso painting had been found on a rubbish tip in London, not too far from the Rothschild house, and had been taken to Vine Street police station.

The next day I was on the phone to Miranda straight away. I told her what I'd heard and urged her to get in touch with Vine Street police. She did and called me back. Yes, they had found a small Picasso. Yes, it was found in a rubbish tip. But it was not Miranda's, it was claimed by somebody else. So I had seen, psychically, a Picasso – but it was the wrong one!

The odds of two small Picassos going missing in a small area of London at the same time must be about a thousand to one but, I must admit, I was a bit embarrassed. Fortunately Miranda thought it was a huge joke and I promised her that I would not give up looking for her Picasso.

A few days later it turned up – in her mother's bedroom, propped up on a shelf. I knew that the painting had not been in that room at the same time as I was. Someone took it and decided to put it back. Who that person was, was not my business to find out . . .

People often ring me to say they have lost some important article, a piece of jewellery, a document or some such thing and I try to find it for them over the phone. What I do is to tune into that person with all my concentration, then I start to imagine them with the object they have lost. Suddenly, I will see it, so I will say something like, 'I can see a wardrobe in a corner and in the bottom of the wardrobe is a black bag and if you look in there you'll find what you're searching for.'

Nine times out of ten it is there.

There is no great secret in doing this. You can do it too and, with practice, you should find it very useful. It is only a question of trusting your instincts and using your psychic eye.

The psychic eye is your third eye. It is in line with your nose, between your other eyes, but upwards from the bridge of the nose, and this is the outlet for the main psychic force of your body.

Scientists and doctors agree that most of us use just one tenth of our brain, and the experts admit that they do not really know what the other nine-tenths is used for. But in that other nine-tenths, I think, lies the part of us that controls our psychic abilities and, in there, is stored knowledge from previous lives.

After childhood most people shut off the psychic area of their brain, they do not hear what it says or use their psychic eye to see beyond the material world they can actually touch or see with a physical eye.

As a psychic, I do use that other nine-tenths, although doubtless only a tiny part of it. I am using more than most people otherwise I would not be psychic. But I suffer in doing so. I have headaches every day of my life and even my doctor has come to the conclusion it is because I am using that part of the brain. It is who I am, what I am and what I do, it is the work that causes the headaches. In fact, I have never yet met a true psychic who did not suffer from migraines or something similar.

The second source of psychic power in your body is the stomach. The stomach is a very, very sensitive area, the actual fleshy part of the stomach, and that is where you *feel* things psychically. Often, on police cases, I feel things first through my stomach, then the dormant part of my brain becomes active and I see through the psychic eye.

With your psychic eye you see what your ordinary eyes cannot. I am told that when I am working I often press the index finger of my right hand to my psychic eye. I am not conscious of doing so, but it helps me to concentrate, so maybe it will help you to concentrate too.

Let us say you want to find a brooch that you have lost. You know it is in the house somewhere, but it seems to have vanished. First, you must sit down quietly, close your eyes and relax. Put your finger to your psychic eye, concentrate on the object you are trying to find and – here's the difficult bit – push all other thoughts out of your mind. You will find that very hard to do to begin with, but it will become easier with time.

With luck, and practice, images will come into your mind. You will see the brooch in its present environment. For example, hidden at the back of a drawer or lying on a blue carpet. Keep an open mind. If you see a fleeting image which is not what you expect to see, do not dismiss it. Trust it – it is probably the right one. Next time you lose something try using your psychic eye – you may well be surprised by the result.

FIVE

An Eye on The Future

'I bumped into Nella at a party and we got chatting. I'd never met her before and she didn't know me from Adam. I heard her telling a friend of mine about a job he was going to be working on in the future so just as a joke I said, "What's going to happen to me?" I was challenging her, I suppose.

'She looked at me and smiled. Then she told me that I would soon be leaving the country and that I would set up in business abroad. The business I would run over there would be the same business that I was involved in here. She told me that I wouldn't be very happy there and that I could come home to Britain in two years. Finally she told me that before I was fifty – I was in my mid-forties at the time – I would have another child.

'I was a bit taken aback. I ran a pub in London with my brother and just days before I had signed the documents to take over a bar in Spain. I was moving out there with my wife, daughter and son-in-law.

'At the time I was confident it was all going to work out fine and we would live happily-ever-after in the sunshine. As for the baby . . . my wife had just had a hysterectomy, I already had three lovely daughters and a bigger family was definitely *not* on the agenda! So I told her she was talking absolute rot!

'After that I forgot all about Nella. It wasn't until I came back to England two years later that I remembered all she had told me.

'The Spanish life hadn't worked out as I had hoped. My daughter and son-in-law were homesick and came back to England, then my wife came back and finally I returned to England too. My marriage broke up, I met someone else and last December my new wife gave birth to our baby girl. I was 48!

'Nella had been right on all counts and when I was back in the country I contacted her. Since then she has told me amazing things that she could not possibly have known about, things about my business, my personal life, my future. I mean, she has told me things that I didn't even know myself. And everything she has told me has eventually come true.

'I'm a born sceptic. I'm a practical man so don't ask me how she does it. I haven't got a clue! All I can say is that Nella can see into the future. That's a fact. It's totally baffling but it's true.'

TONY DUNN, BUSINESSMAN
LONDON, 1992

The fear started to gnaw at me one cold Thursday morning in January and by lunchtime I thought I was going out of my mind.

A bomb – 9.10 a.m. – Heathrow. But where in Heathrow? Which plane? Which day? I was so jittery I did not want to be alone, so I rang a friend who lives up the road and asked her to come in and sit with me.

'Whatever's wrong?' she said. 'You look like a washed out rag. Sit down and I'll make you a nice cup of tea.'

But I couldn't sit down, I couldn't rest. I had to do something. The awful feeling of dread was so familiar to me I knew I couldn't ignore it. It had started when I woke up thinking about another friend of mine who was flying to Zurich from Heathrow the following day. Suddenly I knew he should not go. It was too dangerous and, as the day wore on, the feeling of dread got worse and worse.

In the evening I could not wait any longer. I phoned him and I didn't beat about the bush.

'Please don't get on that plane tomorrow,' I said. 'Please don't go.'

'What's the matter with you?' he said anxiously.

'Is your flight at 9.10?'

'No,' he said.

'Is there a flight at 9.10?'

'Not as far as I know. What's the matter?'

'There's a bomb,' I said. 'Someone has a bomb at the airport. They're trying to put it on an aeroplane.'

He knows me well enough by now to trust what I say and he promised to cancel his flight. That made me feel a little better but the fear would not go away. I couldn't make up my mind what to do next. I could, of course, ring the police. I had done it often enough before and they always take me seriously but, by the time they got through to Heathrow, it might be too late.

In the end I rang another friend of mine who runs his own airline, Das Airlines, from Gatwick Airport, a chap called Captain Joe Roy.

'Joe,' I said. 'You can get through to security quicker than I can. Alert Heathrow. Tell them there's someone at the airport who's waiting to put a bomb on an aeroplane.'

'Right,' he said sounding worried. 'I'll get on to them straight away.'

'Promise?'

'Promise,' and he hung up.

By then I could see them, I could see the bombers both at Heathrow and I could see the bomb. I could also see two place names: Zurich and Frankfurt. The bomb was destined for a plane going to Zurich or Frankfurt, I was sure of it.

There were two of them, a man and a woman, both IRA. The woman was in her early forties, slim with a very thin nose and straight hair which she pulled back away from her face. She was wearing a

95

blue-grey three-quarter length coat, a blue skirt and flattish shoes. The description of the man was not so clear to me.

They were working together but they kept apart. He acted as lookout, checking all the time that she wasn't being watched, because she was the one with the bomb. I kept seeing something white, maybe it was her bag, and in the bag there was something that looked like a hairdryer – except it wasn't a hairdryer – it was packed full of Semtex.

I could see her walking around the terminal building, looking at the flights on the board. Frankfurt. Zurich. Waiting, while the man watched.

The bomb was primed and ready. It would go off at 9.10 a.m. precisely.

Then, as the night wore on, the picture I was seeing began to change. Early on Friday morning I saw policemen. Lots of them. The woman was getting anxious, the man too. He made contact with her and warned her, she was being watched.

They decided to abandon the plan and leave Heathrow. I could see them leaving the terminal building, they got into a car and drove back into London, the bomb still packed in the hairdryer still in her bag. . . . Then I lost them. I could not see any more.

At ten o'clock on Friday morning I turned on the radio. An IRA bomb had exploded in Whitehall, just yards away from 10 Downing Street and within sight of the Houses of Parliament – at 9.10 a.m.

Thank God, no one was hurt, but I am still convinced that the bomb was really intended for an aircraft flying to Zurich or Frankfurt. The terrorists changed their plans at the last moment and left it in a car in Whitehall instead. They sensed the increase in security and the whole business was too risky because it's vital for the IRA that these two are not caught.

They are top terrorists. They are totally professional, deadly, clever, but, more than that, they are so respectable, so very British, no one in the world would suspect them. And that makes them very valuable indeed.

It wasn't the first time I've 'seen' a bomb. I remember years ago on a warm sunny summer's day in 1974, the police collected me in another of their unmarked cars because they wanted me to help them with the case of a little girl who had gone missing and was later found murdered.

We were driving through central London and, as we went past the Tower of London, I jumped in my seat.

'Oh!'

'What is it Nella,' said Dave, the police inspector who was with me.

'I saw the Tower shake.'

I had. It looked as if we were driving through some kind of earthquake and the Old Tower was being shaken to its very foundations. We drove on and I thought no more about it until a few days later a bomb exploded outside the Tower of London.

It is very hard to explain what experiencing clairvoyance actually feels like to someone who has not been through it themselves. Sometimes it is a very worrying experience and I feel ill for days afterwards. Often the feelings become stronger and more intense the closer in time I get to the event. With the Whitehall bomb, as we approached the day and the time, there were several times when I thought I was going to pass out. That is how strong the feeling was. But, when I felt I'd done everything humanly possible to stop it, the feelings eased away and I felt much more relaxed.

Sometimes it is like a video film, moving pictures somehow superimposed onto the ordinary pictures of the everyday life in front of me. Sometimes there is another voice talking to me, as if someone is standing at my shoulder telling me what lies ahead.

Or, maybe, it sounds like my own voice, not coming from within myself, but echoing back to me from a long way away, from somewhere beyond my physical body. Then it is as if there are two people, two Nellas, if you like. There is this Nella, the one you know, the one you can see and talk to. And there is the other Nella, the spiritual Nella.

The first Nella, the Nella you know, is a very ordinary woman, a mum, a granny, a woman like any other with the needs, dreams and hopes of any ordinary woman.

The other Nella is the Nella who can be doing the ironing when, suddenly, she knows that this or that is going to happen. Or she can be talking to someone and suddenly know, with absolute certainty, that this person will soon marry or come into money or break their heart or soon cross to the other side.

I do not fool myself. I know that this is the Nella most people want to meet! They find her much more fascinating than the other one and I can't say I blame them. Because we are all looking for answers, there is nothing more interesting to each and every one of us than the answer to the question 'What is going to happen to me?'

I have only been working as a professional clairvoyant for about fifteen years. Before that I was giving clairvoyance when and where I felt like it and when I heard the voices and knew I had messages I must pass on.

Clairvoyance is very different from my healing work. If I am healing I pray to God to help the patient. With clairvoyance I don't pray. God has given me the gift and it is up to me to use it properly, not to ask Him for more. It is up to me whether I sort out a particular job or not.

My clients come from all walks of life. Our local dustman is a regular but there's a Pakistan royal who comes often too. Sometimes, of course, you can't help recognising a famous face but I accept all clients on an anonymous basis. When they book an appointment I give them a time and that is how I know them from then on. They become Mr Three O'clock or Mrs Five-Thirty.

Strangely enough, some people, often celebrities, are rather put out if you are not interested in their famous names. They want you to know who they are and, I suppose, to be impressed.

One Spring morning I was admiring the crocuses outside my sitting room window when a London taxi drew up outside my house and a large black gentleman got out. It was obvious he was in a state of absolute panic.

'I need your help,' he said.

I told him to come in and tried to calm him down. He introduced himself as the former president of a large African country. For some reason, he obviously thought I wouldn't believe this and went on to produce, from every pocket, documents to prove his identity.

'See,' he said. 'My passport. My visas. My driving licences.'

I said, 'I don't care if you're Joe Bloggs from down the road. It makes no odds to me.'

We sat down and I gave him a reading. Mostly he wanted insight into the political situation in his country. He wanted to get back into power but he was going the wrong way about it.

After that he came to see me regularly and I helped him as much as I could but, whatever I advised him, he would always do the exact opposite! I could see that if he did such-and-such a thing and such-and-such another thing he would be reinstated as President. I could see him as President in my mind's eye.

But he didn't take my advice. I could see that a big British organisation was funding one of his rivals; I could see the meetings. So I told him, 'You've got to get in there and see them and you should say this and that.' But he didn't, and now he is a barrister in New York!

He rings me occasionally from there and often says, 'Nella, I wish I'd taken your advice.' I do too. He gave me a document that said if he was ever reinstated as President I was to have a quarter of a million pounds in return for all my help!

Politicians, I have found, are always desperate for advice and frantic to find out what is going to happen in their future. But they are the people least likely to believe you if what you say doesn't suit their hopes and they are the least likely to heed your advice!

Another African politician who came to see me several times and thank heavens he, at least, *did* listen to my advice. The situation in his country was very volatile at the time and he wanted to know if there was any danger around him because he was travelling home on the following Thursday.

The spiritual Nella said, 'Tell this man he must not travel on Thursday but it will be safe for him to travel at the weekend.'

So I passed the message on. I knew that if he travelled on Thursday there would be gunmen waiting for him at the other end. As it turned out, that is exactly what happened. He did not travel, there were gunmen waiting for him, and my warning saved his life.

Then he asked me if he would keep his seat in Government

because, like most politicians, he was worried he was about to get kicked out. I said, 'Go back now and your seat will be safe,' and it was.

At the same time he told me that his wife was very ill so I gave him a chiffon scarf I was wearing at the time and I put it in an envelope. I said, 'You must promise that you will not touch this scarf, and you won't let anyone else touch it, except your wife. She is to wear it until she feels better.'

Off he went, back to Africa, and a week or so later I was sent a message that his wife was better.

I don't know how these people get to hear about me. Maybe it is word of mouth, or they read about me and one of my cases in the newspapers. One day it was a member of the Pakistani royal family who was standing there on the doorstep, the next it was a famous American author.

After I had finished his reading he said, 'Do you know who I am?'

'No,' I said.

And he told me he was the author of many world-wide bestselling novels.

'That's nice,' I said and he gave me his card and asked me to visit him and his wife in America.

Usually, once a reading is over, I forget what I have told a client. The words come out and I forget instantly. But, if the words linger awhile and I do remember, I always keep that to myself. All my readings are totally confidential. If I broke that confidentiality it would break the entire chain of what I do, so there would be no point. Besides, sometimes I pick up events that are so private it would not be right for anyone else to be told.

There is nothing I keep back. Whether what I see is good or bad, I tell, and I make that quite clear to my client from the start. The other thing I stress is that if I cannot pick up anything for them, nothing of any substance, I will tell them so. I will not charge them and they will have to make a new appointment for another day. That can happen sometimes, especially when I am tired. I try to see the pictures but there is nothing. I listen for the voices – nothing. Silence.

I can usually sense immediately if I'm going to get anything or not and then I say, 'Whether I get good news or bad you're going to hear it.'

Most people say, 'Fine.' But some people complain.

They say, 'I don't want to hear anything bad.'

To them I say, 'I'm sorry, I can't pick out the bits you want to hear and leave out the bits you don't want to hear.'

I don't mean to be unsympathetic. I am not unsympathetic. I know how upsetting it can be if you are told that life is not going to turn out as you had hoped – I *feel* the pain of what may happen as I talk and I have had many people actually leave the house in tears. But, whenever that has happened, they have either phoned later or come back to visit again and they have always said, 'Nella, you were right.'

People may be upset by what I tell them, not because their future looks bleak, but because they are hoping someone else will act in a certain way – maybe declare undying love or offer them a job – and I can't see the other person doing that. That is what distresses them although often, later, on reflection, they can see that it all turned out for the best.

I remember one recent case in particular. A group of nurses from Guy's Hospital used to come down to me regularly for clairvoyance and one Friday morning I got a call from them.

This was unusual because they usually came earlier in the week as they knew that Friday nights were reserved for my healing sessions. All they told me was, 'Nella, we've got a friend who's in terrible trouble. Can we bring her down to see you?'

The answer, of course, was yes, and down they came to Bexleyheath. The poor girl they brought with them was in floods of tears but she said nothing. She certainly didn't tell me why she was so upset, she just sat there and cried.

I looked at her and I felt happiness.

'I don't know why you're crying, darling,' I said. 'You'll be married within three months. You won't marry here, you'll marry in South Africa.'

As I said that she stood up and stormed out. The girls said, 'Oh, Nella.'

I was surprised. 'What's the matter?'

Then they told me she had been courting a man for eight years and he had just told her that he was marrying someone else the following day. No wonder she was devastated.

But I still felt happy about that young girl and rightly, as it turned out. Two months went past and I received a lovely postcard from South Africa.

In an attempt to cheer her up the other nurses had taken their friend out to a wine bar where she had bumped into an old college friend. They had been boyfriend and girlfriend years before but had lost touch. Now they took one look at each other, fell instantly in love and since his parents lived in South Africa they had gone out there to get married. It really made my day!

It is lovely for me when I see happiness on its way to someone because I see so much sadness and despair in my work. When I am working with the police to find a murderers that person's evil seeps into my mind and it is hard to shake off. And in my healing work I see such great courage; but always there is struggle, the struggle to be well, the struggle to cope, to stay cheerful. So, it gives me a great boost when the moving pictures are showing me joy and the voices are telling me, 'This person may not be happy now Nella, but in two weeks, in two months . . .'

No clairvoyant of any repute would ever tell anyone that they were dying or would die soon. If anyone claiming to be clairvoyant ever tells you that, dismiss it as pure rubbish and leave and, for God's sake, don't worry about it.

Death is the only certainty, death comes to us all, but how and when is not for us to know and it is certainly not for any clairvoyant to say. Besides the immorality of making such a prophesy, it is difficult for even the most brilliant clairvoyant to know. It is certainly true that sometimes I look at someone and know that soon they will be moving on, but death doesn't always convey itself to the clairvoyant as a feeling of pain, anguish or despair.

I remember one case, not a criminal case, in which I was asked by some people to find out what had happened to a child. They did not know where the child was, or even whether he was alive or dead.

As I concentrated on this little boy I felt enormous happiness and peace, such a warm and wonderful sensation, that I said I was sure he must be alive and happy. I found out later he was dead. He had died of natural causes and his family had buried him in a cemetery, in hallowed ground. He was at peace and what I had felt was the peace and happiness of his innocent little spirit.

If my pictures do show me troubles ahead I will always try and warn the person if it is something that is avoidable, like an accident. I'll say, 'Don't drive your car on that day,' or 'Don't fly in an aircraft on that day.'

Once I met a young man and I knew as soon as I saw him that, if he wasn't careful, he would shortly be involved in a car accident. I told him, 'Don't drive your car this coming Sunday.' Anyway, either he took no notice of me, or he forgot, and he went off driving on the Sunday. When he got to a roundabout his steering locked and he found himself hurtling towards a lampost. In those split seconds, he remembered what I had told him and threw himself sideways across the passenger seat. His life was saved.

I don't believe that giving a warning like that is cheating death. In the end no one can cheat death. I believe that much of the path we walk to that ultimate destination is predestined, but incidents along the way are not. If you heed warnings, you will still fulfil your destiny. You have a time and a place to die. You won't die until you reach that place and that time arrives.

My warning – and heeding my warning – is as much predestined as anything else.

When I finish working I try my best to turn off the pictures and the voices but, if you have developed your psychic power, you can never close yourself off from clairvoyance entirely. You can do it with one particular job but you cannot close the psychic eye altogether. You can be washing up, watching television, doing the shopping and suddenly, if you are clairvoyant like me, you get flashes of what is going to happen, like a video on fast forward.

Years ago I was at home cleaning and cooking, when suddenly I 'saw' Prince Charles. I had a terrible feeling of disaster and the picture was very clear. I was so worried I rang a police officer who was a friend of mine and said to him, 'I'm very worried about Prince Charles.' He didn't laugh at me. Most of my friends, and most of the police I have worked with, don't laugh at me or my visions. They've discovered that, all too often, they turn out to be true.

'I'm worried,' I said. 'He's in great danger.'

My friend put me in touch with Chief Inspector Reese, who was then in charge of the police force at Buckingham Palace, and he came down to see me. The image I was getting was still very strong in my mind and I told him, 'What I'm seeing is this . . . Prince Charles is walking beside a very fair man. His hair is very, very fair. They are walking in a kind of open space and there's bunting up everywhere and there are lots of tents. There's noise and people and in the centre is a long marquee with fancy edges to it.'

I told Chief Inspector Reese that I could see him there too. 'And when you go into that marquee a very short Italian man will come up to you and say, "What would you like to drink, sir." In that marquee there is great danger. There are two IRA men there, one of them is wearing a brown jacket, and they have a bomb. They are there because they don't believe there is going to be heavy security surrounding the event.'

I felt better once I had told Chief Inspector Reese. I always feel better when I know I have to warn someone of something and I manage to do so. The police rarely come back and tell me how right or wrong I have been. I usually get the feedback in a roundabout way. They come and see me about another case and say, 'Oh, by the way, Nella you were absolutely spot on with that other job.'

But, in this case, I am pleased to say that the Chief Inspector did take the time to phone me and tell me what had happened.

'Nella,' he said. 'You freaked my men out about this job.' It turned out that Prince Charles had one official engagement some days after I met the Chief Inspector. Security was arranged as usual for that event but, what the police weren't told was that, he had decided to go to another charity event organised by Jimmy Saville at very short notice.

Prince Charles walked into the field with Jimmy Saville – a celebrity famous for his blond-white hair. There they met Chief Inspector Reese. As he walked into a marquee, with decorative edging around the entrance, he was asked by a small Italian waiter, 'What would you like to drink, sir.'

The police caught no IRA men that day but I am still convinced they were there until the inspector's men made themselves visible in the area where I had instructed him to beef-up security, and the bombers made a hasty retreat. As far as I know Prince Charles carried on unaware of any panic and I was satisfied that I had done my best.

For me, it is far worse to see accidents, murders or terrible tragedies in my mind, but be unable to see the whole picture, or sufficient details, to be able to prevent them.

In early Spring 1987 I was working with two private investigators in the North of England and we were driving around in their car looking for a missing person. It was a fairly routine sort of case. By now, I am used to the fact that sometimes electrical instruments, like kettles, televisions or electric typewriters, behave very peculiarly when I am around. But on this occasion even I thought what happened was very weird. I was sitting in the car with these two chaps when suddenly the radio went off. The two men could not understand it. They looked at it, fiddled with it, thumped it and then I said, 'I think I know what's the matter with it. It's me.'

We stopped the car and I told them to keep the radio switched on even though it wasn't working but was making a strange crackling sound. When I got out of the car the radio came on again. When I got back in the car the radio went off. I got out, it went on. I got in, it went off.

I knew then that there was a tremendous electrical charge coming from me that day and suddenly I had an overwhelming feeling of fear. 'Don't go to Belgium,' I told them. They had said earlier in the day there was a case in Belgium they were going to work on.

'Don't go to Belgium.'

'Why not, Nella?'

'I don't know. But I know neither of you must go.'

I couldn't see the pictures clearly but I knew their journey to Belgium would lead them into great danger. I felt swamped by fear. I would not stop warning them. A voice kept saying to me, 'Nella, don't let them go, don't let them go.'

They didn't go. They were due to cross the channel by ferry to Zeebrugge but they didn't go, thank God. The ship they would have travelled home on was the *Herald of Free Enterprise*. Outside Zeebrugge she went down and almost 200 people drowned.

Those two years were a terrible time in our country. One major disaster after another shocked us all. First there was the *Herald of Free Enterprise*. Then there was the Clapham rail disaster in which a train packed with commuters on their way to London's Waterloo station crashed outside Clapham Junction, the busiest railway junction in the world.

Later that day I was on the phone to Ellie, a friend of mine from TV AM, the morning TV station where I worked every week.

'Nella,' she said. 'Isn't the train crash awful? I really cried when I heard what had happened.'

'Well, don't put your handkerchief away yet, love,' I said.

'What do you mean?'

'There's worse to come,' I said.

'Another train crash?'

'No, this one's a plane crash north of England.'

It was almost Christmas and everywhere there were lights and singing. I would walk along the streets as, like everyone else, I did my

Christmas shopping, and I would admire the little Christmas trees in people's windows and stop and listen to the local school children singing carols in the High Street. But I didn't feel in a festive mood. I could not shake off that familiar feeling of dread and for days I had been seeing snatches of a moving picture.

A plane was exploding, crashing, there was fire, there were pieces of metal all over the ground. I smelled death.

The picture would come to me from time to time throughout the day and the feeling of death, shock and despair, was terrible. I just wanted to push it away from me. I kept trying to push it all out of my vision. I didn't want to see this terrible sight, I didn't want these feelings. I wanted a normal happy family Christmas.

Just four days later, on December 21, 1988, Pan Am Flight 103, travelling from Frankfurt to New York via Heathrow, exploded in mid-air and crashed in a fireball onto the small town of Lockerbie on the Scottish borders.

Every passenger, and there were nearly three hundred of them on the jumbo jet, was killed, and many others died in Lockerbie on the ground. It was Britain's worst air disaster and among the ten worst the world has ever seen.

Of course everyone was devastated, especially those poor families. I felt guilty. If only I had not pushed the pictures away. If only I had concentrated. If only I had tried to see the number of the side of the plane or, at least, the name of the airline, perhaps I could have stopped it and saved those people. But that wasn't to be.

So, there are times when I want to push what I see away from me – sometimes it is about someone I love dearly. The images begin to form but I consciously give those pictures a big shove in the opposite direction. The feeling begins in my solar plexus and I can feel whether it's going to be good or bad and that is just what I don't want to know. If I was forever using clairvoyance with my nearest and dearest, life would be intolerable.

But, of course, there are exceptions. I still chuckle to myself when I remember my first meetings with my son-in-law Karl, who was working in computers. My daughter, Gaynor, was going out with a friend of his but Karl often used to pop around to my house for a chat.

He said to me once, 'Do you think Gaynor will marry my friend?'

'No,' I said. 'I don't think so.'

'Well, who do you think she'll marry?'

I said, 'I think she'll marry someone about your size Karl. He'll have brown, straight hair.'

'You don't know who it is, do you?' he asked.

I smiled. 'You'll have to wait and see.'

I knew he was the one all along but it would have been wrong to say. I am ashamed to admit that I used to wind him up really badly and now he often says to me, 'You were describing me, weren't you?'

Karl and Gaynor married and a year later Gaynor was pregnant with their first baby.

I was thrilled to bits. I knew it was going to be a boy and I told everyone the date and the time the baby would be born. On the big day – one day earlier than my prediction – Gaynor went into labour and Karl sat with her while his parents and I sat outside waiting, waiting, all evening. Eventually, after a few hours, Karl's mum and dad went home to get something to eat. I was still sitting there in the waiting room when the sister came out and said in that brisk medical way, 'Mrs Jones you might just as well go home, this baby won't be born for hours yet.'

I said, 'I'm not going. The baby will be born soon.'

She was amused. 'Oh you know, do you?'

'Yes,' I said.

'The baby will be born between midnight and 12.15.'

'It won't be born until morning, Mrs Jones.'

'Let's wait and see.'

And, at 12.14, my lovely grandson James entered this world.

Things did not go so well for Gaynor and Karl the second time and, as soon as she told me she was pregnant again, I knew there was something wrong. Of course, I couldn't say anything, but for months I worried and when she was five months pregnant the hospital confirmed that there was a problem with the baby.

I knew the baby was going to be a girl and I said to Gaynor,

'I've known about this and there is going to be a problem, darling, but I also know it's going to be alright. She's going to be OK.'

When our little Katie was born they found she had an extra small kidney growing on top of one of her normal kidneys and there were other complications. When she was just 13 weeks old they operated on her at the world famous children's hospital in Great Ormond Street.

Thank God, the operation was a success and, although she has to take a little antibiotic every night, she is marvellous now, a happy healthy little girl of four.

As I have said, I usually try and push away visions which show future events in the lives of those I know and love.

But equally, just like everyone else, there are times when I would love to be able to see what lay ahead for me personally – the good things, of course!

To a certain extent I can. I know when goodness or badness is coming towards me. I can feel it. And I feel I have some love coming into my life this year, which will be nice! Earlier this year I knew I was going to be ill. I tried to look ahead but all I could see, was black, black, black – but then I rarely see anything in detail for myself. It is far easier to be clairvoyant for other people. Inside me, I hope all the hopes, and dream all the dreams, of any ordinary woman and it would be so very easy to see those, to project those into my mind, because they are the hopes and dreams I want to become reality.

I do believe that you can train yourself to be clairvoyant to a certain extent. Once again it is a question of using that other ninety per cent of your brain that has been sitting there idle for so long. You have also got to be very sensitive, very caring and you must be extremely dedicated, prepared to work at it. It is no good just sitting there doing it for fun, it won't work.

Relaxation is very important. Even if you don't relax your body, you must learn to relax your mind. The mind is more important.

Obviously when I am out working with the police on a case, I can't relax my body. We travel all over the place, meet all sorts of people and sometimes I can find myself traipsing through fields and woods, but I have to relax my mind otherwise I get nothing.

You have to push everything out of your mind, all the bits and bobs of everyday thoughts that are whizzing around, push all of that away and concentrate only on the goal you have set yourself. You have to be literally single-minded. The technique is very similar to meditation, except your are concentrating your thoughts out of yourself rather than within yourself.

This is not an easy task, especially if you have got a scatter-brain like me, one that goes hopping around all over the place. But you can achieve it, as I have done, through sheer determination. If this is what you want, you can do it. But, first, you have to learn to discipline your mind.

Discipline, as well as any instinctive talent you may have, is the key if you want to focus in on some particular subject.

Of course, I am the first to admit that it doesn't always work. There have been many times when I have tried to see what is going to happen in a particular context and, however hard I try, however hard I concentrate, however I discipline my mind, I can see nothing and there are times when I get it wrong. Not often, but it has been known!

Having made that confession, I have to say, in my own defence, that often what I say may appear to be totally off-beam at the time, but the significance of the clues I am given becomes apparent at a later date.

Sometimes it takes years for a prophesy to make sense. In 1979 I kept seeing illness, not for myself or those I knew, but a plague which afflicted whole continents and finally the entire world.

It was not until the mid-eighties that people began to become aware of the danger of AIDS. As soon as I heard it being discussed on the television I knew that it was the plague I had been dreading.

Several times, in recent years, I have felt that someone was trying to tell me about a cure for cancer. It is confused, but I see pictures of a plant under the sea. It looks like a sea cucumber or a sea slug, that's the shape of it. I have a very strong feeling that a cure for cancer will be found and that a plant from beneath the oceans will be the secret to its success. And I believe we shall see that happening in the relatively near future.

Then the big killer will be AIDS. At the moment the authorities seem to be playing down the AIDS epidemic but I think it is going to get worse and I do not see a cure yet, at least not in my lifetime.

More and more these days I find that I am being forced to save my gift, the force, the power, whatever it is, for the important work. I must not throw it away. I must not waste it. It is precious. So there are some situations I avoid as far as possible.

For example, I loathe the world of politics. Obviously, when a politician comes to see me for a reading, I treat them in the same way as everyone else and tell them what I see. But I do not enjoy being dragged into the realms of political forecasts. I am not some sort of psychic National Opinion Poll. That is not what my gift is for.

Many people contacted me during the last General Election but I refused to get involved. In fact, I find it quite difficult to give clairvoyance for politicians. They are usually only interested in their political ambitions but, invariably, I pick up different things entirely.

In 1987 I was asked, on a live television programme, to predict who was going to win that general election. I knew Mrs Thatcher would win but, as soon as I started to concentrate on her, I received different messages that had nothing to do with politics.

I told the audience that she would win but that after her victory she would be out of action for a while because of illness. Even after the show was over the feeling stayed with me and grew stronger. So much so that I told a reporter there that I was sure that the illness was going to affect her head.

Margaret Thatcher did, of course, win that election and very shortly afterwards she had to have an operation on one of her eyes for a detached retina.

In the late 1970s I predicted the Gulf War. Even when the Cold War was at its chilliest I knew that there would never be a nuclear war between America and Russia, but I continually saw a war in a Middle Eastern country.

During the Gulf War I followed the news on television like everyone else. But, for me, it was *déjà vu*, a re-run of all the images I had seen with my psychic eye years earlier. Unfortunately those images have not yet run their full course. I am sure the conflict with Iraq is not yet over.

People who meet me are often surprised that I'm not a millionairess! After all, they say, if I can see into the future why can't I foretell which horse is going to win the Grand National or which numbers are going to come up on the pools?

I probably could, but that is not the purpose of my gift. I simply know that I cannot use my gift in that way. It would not be right – so don't ever come to see me asking me to give you numbers for the pools, because I won't!

I have only done that once. A few years ago a police inspector friend and the lads at his station got together in a pools syndicate. Every time I saw him he would pester me for the right numbers for the pools so he and his mates could make a million!

He went on and on until finally I was so fed up with him I said, 'OK, I will do this once and once only.' I gave him a list of numbers and told him to follow them every week for six weeks.

The syndicate did as I said for five weeks. In the sixth week most of them went to the Hendon Police Training College to lecture young constables just joining the force. The one police officer who was left behind at the station foolishly changed my numbers to some of his own and, of course, that week my numbers came up! The payout was enormous. I am surprised that young police officer is still alive!

'Do it again, Nella,' begged my police friend.

But I told him, 'You had your chance. I gave them to you once. I'm not giving them to you twice.'

I have to confess that I have used my gift with the pools to raise a little extra cash for myself, but I have only done it twice and only when I was really stony broke.

The first time I was living in a flat in Charlton, Gaynor was small and I was so badly off financially that I could not even afford to buy her a pair of new shoes. So I sat down and did the pools. I did not think about football or numbers. I cleared my mind completely and said aloud to whoever was listening on the other side, 'I wouldn't ask but I am desperate . . .'

That week I won £400.

I did it again shortly after I moved to this house in Bexleyheath. I sat at the dining room table and I didn't ask for much, just enough to see me through a very difficult time.

That week I won £800.

I have never tried it again and I never will. Like everyone else I have sometimes thought about what I would do if I won a million pounds on the pools. We all fantasise, don't we? I would travel, head off to the sunshine, maybe enjoy a nice long cruise around the world.

But I know for sure it won't happen. I do not believe that is my destiny. I am only human and, if I had all that money, would I continue with my healing work? Would I carry on every day with my work of helping other people cope with their problems in this life? I don't know. Somehow I don't think so. The temptation to merely go off and enjoy myself might be too strong!

I am not used to money and I believe my destiny in this life is to use my gift to help others, not to make a lot of money for myself and live a life of luxury and self-indulgence. I have come to accept that, though, I have to admit, somewhat reluctantly!

SIX

Things that Go Bump . . .

'From ghoulies and ghosties and long-leggety beasties
And things that go bump in the night,
Good Lord, deliver us!'

AN OLD CORNISH SAYING,
ANONYMOUS

The old farm house was enchanting with its faded red brick, white lath-and-plaster, dark, sturdy oak beams and moss clinging to the slate roof. Since the sixteenth century it had sat here surrounded by its classic English garden, comfortably at home in the green hills of Kent.

But, as soon as I got to the gate, I knew I did not want to go in. I shivered, not because of the frost in the early morning air, but because, for the first time in many years, I was truly afraid. I stood there, glued to the spot, dreading that walk up the pretty cobbled path to the front door, and I kept hearing the words in my head, 'Turn around Nella, go away, go home.'

The house was owned by a young man and his wife who worked as a nursing sister at the local hospital. They were a lovely couple with two beautiful children, a happy family living in this wonderful house in an idyllic setting. Everything should have been perfect. But there was something, or someone, living in the house with them and making their lives absolute hell.

In desperation, the couple had called me and begged me to visit them in the hope that, maybe, I could lay this malevolent spirit and persuade it to leave them alone.

They told me that the ghost showed no interest in the young man or, thank God, the children. It had set its sights firmly on the young mother and wouldn't leave her alone until now, after some months, the whole experience was making her physically ill.

At night, in bed, she would sense it as a heavy black weight pushing her down, down, down. Or, she would feel hands trying to drag her out of bed. During the day she could feel its presence as it followed her around the house and then, suddenly, it would throw her against the wall or into the fire.

I had agreed to help but I honestly think that if the couple hadn't spotted me through the window, and opened the door to welcome me, I would have chickened out and run away – the feeling of menace about that place was so strong. But the poor woman had seen me so I had to go in and, as I slowly made my way up the path, I knew that someone else was also watching my arrival with interest.

Inside the house was equally lovely. We went into a big sitting room with a wonderful inglenook fireplace you could walk right into. The children had been sent off to spend the day with their grandma and I stood by the fireplace talking to the woman about what had been happening.

But, as we were chatting, I had a sense that upstairs, immediately above me, he was waiting for me. It was a terrible feeling, an awful weight of apprehension. I couldn't settle, just standing there. I carried on talking but I was rambling really, I didn't know what I was saying. All I could think of was the 'thing' above me.

I said, 'Excuse me, does this thing appear in the room above this?'

'Yes, that's my bedroom,' she said.

'Well,' I said, 'let's get this over and done with.' And with heavy feet I walked up the stairs.

Although the ghost concentrated all his attention on the young mother she was not the only one who had seen the mysterious shape. Her husband had seen it, the babysitter had seen it, lots of people had seen it.

I opened the bedroom door and told the others to stay on the landing but to keep the door open so they could see what was going on. Frankly, I didn't want them to be too far away for my own sake.

Inside, the room seemed full of mist; a thick, white foggy mist, and I felt I had to go and stand with my back against a certain part of the wall.

The woman cried out, 'Oh my God! That's where this thing appears every night.'

I started to pray aloud. I tried to say the Lord's Prayer but I could not get the words out. I felt the words being snatched away from me. I had been saying that prayer every day of my life but I couldn't remember the words. By now I was getting panicky. I forced myself to calm my thoughts. I thought, 'Careful Nella, this thing is getting at you. This thing is taking you over.'

I could feel my energy, my very lifeforce, being sapped out of me. It was dreadful, but I forced myself to keep going. 'Please God help me, please God help me,' and, at last, I managed to say the Lord's Prayer all the way through aloud.

Then, over the bed, I saw something begin to take shape. It was moving towards me and I began to be able to make out its facial features. It was a man with a long mass of hair, a beard and its eyes were quite terrifying. They were the eyes of a mad man.

The thing was looking at me with hatred but I took a deep breath and started talking to it. 'You don't belong here any more. God's given you a place and you should be in that place.'

It started gabbling at me and I couldn't make any sense of what it was saying. So I kept on at it. 'You're not supposed to be here. This is not your place. You should be where God has a place for you, you should be in that place.' I would not retreat and I would not stop talking. I wouldn't give it a break. Then, I started praying for this thing, this spirit. I was praying hard and loud, 'God, take care of this spirit, this soul.'

I was shaking as I prayed but it seemed to calm him down. Everything went quiet and then, when I looked at it, where the eyes had been mad before now there was just great sadness in a man's face.

I said, 'Now tell me why you've come back here? Why are you tormenting this poor woman, the lady of this house? She's done nothing to you.'

Little by little he told me his story. The gabbling stopped and I could understand what he was saying. He had been a sailor, he told me. He'd met and fallen in love with a girl from this village and he planned that, on his next trip home, they were going to be married and live in this house.

He went away to sea but when he came back he discovered that his brother had married the girl and they had moved into the same house he had hoped would be his family home. He went mad, took an axe and killed both of them – his brother and his girl, he murdered them both.

I said to him, 'Do you feel better now? This is not your place, she is not your woman. Go in peace, my friend. Let your spirit go in peace.' As he went, all the mist in the room cleared. It had been cold in that room before but, immediately, it began to feel warmer.

The poor man had been tormenting the woman because, in his demented mind, it was the same woman who had betrayed him. Now he saw it was not the same woman he could leave her with her own family and it was a great relief to his tortured spirit.

For me the encounter was a terrifying experience, as it was for those who watched it. A photographer was there on the landing with the young couple, a big burly man he was, but he had to run outside because he was physically sick with fear. The photographer had brought a tape recorder with him and he taped the whole episode. When we played it back, at the time that the spirit faded away and the mist in the room cleared, it was very strange. You could hear on the tape the sound of a man heaving an enormous sigh. I think that spirit was just as happy to be free of that house at last, and the unhappy memories it held for him, as the young family were to see him go.

I will never forget that day. It is one of the few times I have ever been frightened of a ghost or spirit. I never underestimate the powers of some spirits and I can see, when they are misunderstood, how they can frighten people, but mostly I have welcomed them into my life.

The ghosts I saw as a child were lovely. I wasn't frightened at all. I found them very comforting. I've seen spirits on and off all my life. You look around and suddenly they are there and, maybe, they stay awhile and maybe they don't and then they are gone.

Usually they are the spirits of people I don't know, although I have seen the spirit of my mother a couple of times. She doesn't look like she did when she was here on Earth, she looks much younger. Some ghosts appear as they did when they were on Earth but I think most of them appear in the way they best remember themselves.

Every house I have ever lived in has been haunted and I'm sure that most houses have got some kind of spirit in them. You can feel it when you walk in and you'll know if it's a friendly or unfriendly spirit by the atmosphere in the house. When I first bought my house here in Bexleyheath it was a total wreck – no floors, hardly any ceilings and all the plaster coming off the walls. It was just a shell of a house but I knew, as soon as I walked in, that the spirits here were friendly to me. They welcomed me into the house and were happy that I had chosen this place as my home.

Whenever you're buying a house, always trust you first instincts when you walk in. Forget the decor, sense the atmosphere, trust what you feel and if that's a good feeling you know you'll be happy in that house.

Many people are terrified of ghosts but people have always been frightened of things they don't understand and, of course, there are those who deny their existence. I can only say to them that they are wrong. On the other side of the coin are the many thousands of people who believe in ghosts, who would love to see one, but never do. It's bad luck that the more you want to see one, the more you go out of your way to see them, the less likely it is for one to show itself!

You can't demand that a ghost appear before you. It won't. But I do believe that anyone can see a ghost as long as they are, at that particular time, in a receptive mood and not merely willing a ghost to appear. Your mind is like a radio receiver and transmitter; your mind must be open, the switch must be set to 'On'. You have to be on the wavelength where you're receptive to the spirits around you.

A ghost is someone who has physically died and come back in spirit form. They do not necessarily come back for any particular purpose. If they love someone, or they love a particular place and they were happy there in their earthly lives, they may come back to that person or that place again and again.

Some spirits don't realise immediately that they are dead. They still walk the Earth thinking that they are alive. That usually happens in cases of very sudden death such as a motor accident or air crash. It has all happened so quickly they do not realise that they don't belong on the Earth any more, that their place is on the other side. But there are always other spirits, highly evolved, understanding spirits, who will finally guide them to the place where they should rightly be.

People who have recently lost someone they love often tell me that they feel that person around them. They still feel them in the house or expect to see them walking round the corner. Sometimes, they say, they especially feel their presence when they are crying over their loss. Unfortunately, these people are often told by the sceptics to ignore these feelings, they must face up to the reality of the death. They say, bluntly, that the person is never coming back and those who are left behind have got to get on with their own lives without clinging to the belief that the loved one is still there. The bereaved are told it is all in their imagination.

I believe this is simply not true. I believe that spirits often come back to comfort the people they love and have left. It's the love-link again and, if there is that love-link, it cannot be broken by death. That love-link goes on forever.

I don't believe it does us any harm to talk to the spirits of our dead loved ones. In fact, most of us find ourselves doing just that without even thinking about it. A widow will suddenly find herself saying,

'OK, George,' or whatever her husband's name was, 'where did you put the garden shears?' And she'll suddenly find them.

Or, someone who has lost their mother will find himself saying to the dead parent, 'I wish you were here to help me through this, Mum.' You say it without thinking because subconsciously you know that Mum is there and she will help you.

But you cannot make them appear at will. You can't say, 'Come on, show yourself now,' as many modern ghostbusters do, especially the ones who are trying to disprove that ghosts exist. Spirits will only appear in their own time and when your mind is receptive to them. The spirits are probably here much of the time but they are only back on Earth because they chose to come back and they will only appear when they choose to appear.

Some ghosts are mischievous and they only come back to have some fun. Most of these are spirits of young people, often children or teenagers. They like making mischief without having any earthly restrictions on them.

If you can imagine a mischievous child in spirit, there is no mother to say, 'I'll smack your bottom if you're not a good boy – or girl.'

So they think, 'This is great. We'll go back and we can do just as we like and there's no one to scold us or smack us or punish us! Brilliant!'

Then they start doing naughty things like frightening unsuspecting victims out of their lives by making furniture apparently move on its own!

If you are lucky enough to see a ghost the experience will probably give you a real boost. I have my own favourite ghost, a monk at Bexley Abbey, whom I visit regularly and, without fail, I return from our meetings feeling refreshed and uplifted.

I first saw him about eight years ago. It was a very ordinary evening at home. It was November, the evenings were drawing in and our lodger, Uncle Jack, was sitting watching television while I sewed name tags in Gaynor's school clothes.

Suddenly I thought, 'Just a minute, put this down, Nella. You've got to go somewhere.'

I told Gaynor and Uncle Jack I had to go out for a while. It was half-past nine on a winter's night but I got in the car and drove down to Bexley Abbey. I did not know why I had to drive to the Abbey, I just knew that I had to do it. It was as if someone had called me.

When I got there, I stood outside the Abbey and waited in the dark. It was not long before he appeared: a monk wearing a black habit with a big hood pulled down so I couldn't see his face, and he kept his arms hidden in his big sleeves.

He doesn't walk, he glides. The Abbey is all in ruins now but there is an archway still standing and that is always where I catch my first glimpse of him. He comes out of the archway and walks along a high wall, then he turns towards me.

Every time I see him I try to speak to him but I am always disappointed. Before he reaches me, he turns and appears to glide down some steps. In fact, I've looked at the place in the cold light of day and there are no steps in that position but they must have been there at one time because that is where and how he always appears.

I do not know if he is aware of my presence. I think he probably is, although I never see his face. He always stays for a good few minutes – he doesn't appear and disappear in a second. To this day I am still not sure why I felt compelled to go to the Abbey. Obviously it was to see him, but why? The only explanation I can think of is that whenever I do see him I feel good. It's a fantastic experience and, for days afterwards, I feel stronger and more cheerful. Perhaps his visits are just a treat for me when I have been working hard!

My monk appears to glide along the ground but apart from that he looks completely human, a man of real flesh and blood. Many people imagine that if you see a ghost it will look like the caricature of a ghostly figure, wailing and whooing and wafting about like someone from the Klu Klux Klan!

In fact, usually, they look completely normal, just like you or me. They have arms and legs, they wear clothes, they are human but in spirit form.

If you see only one part of a body without the rest it means that someone is attempting to get through but they haven't got quite enough energy. As they struggle to appear you can see the ectoplasm as a kind of white mist, or sometimes tiny fine dots of light. Then, you might be able to make out the head and shoulders of the person or, sometimes, just the hands.

You will sense a ghost before you see him, or her. If you feel a presence in the room don't disregard it as nothing. Open your mind and accept that someone is trying to get through to you. Maybe you will feel someone blowing on your face, touching you gently on the shoulder or softly stroking your hair. Often, you have an overwhelming impression that someone is standing right behind you, at your shoulder.

Do not be afraid. They want to touch you because there is love there, they want to look after you. If you love someone the most natural instinct in the world is to want to touch them.

If you start thinking of someone who you have loved and lost you may often feel them close to you. Frequently, when I am sitting with someone who has been bereaved the dead person comes through and tells me little everyday things that no one but the two of them could have actually known.

It is as if they are trying to reassure the person still living on this side. They are saying, 'Look, there is life after death. I'm here contacting you and I'm dead as far as you know. But I'm here, I'm fine and I still love you.'

Most people who go to see a clairvoyant or psychic are faced with some major problem, or they are suffering from some heartache or loss. Of course, some people come for a reading out of sheer bravado, almost trying to prove that I am a fake. But spirits often appear despite that and then my visitor usually goes home in a different frame of mind!

Most people find contact with the dead a great comfort. The spirits certainly comfort me. I sense ghosts around all the time and I see them regularly.

There is one I call my 'Guardian Angel' who is always looking over me. I do not know who he is and he has never shown himself to me but I know that he is there to help me. It's nice, it's security.

I never seek out ghosts. I just make myself available and they know that I am a channel they can come through if they want to. There are no restrictions here with me. They can say to me whatever they want to.

Often a ghost will tell me about the mannerisms they had when they were here, on this side. They'll say, 'I used to do this or that,' and they will actually show me the way they walked or whatever. All of us have our own little characteristics. Maybe, they moved their hands in a particular way or they used to flick back their hair in a certain way or I have had one or two who were always rubbing one ear! In spirit they will show me what they did and I'll imitate that mannerism. Then the person I am giving the sitting for usually says, 'Oh God! Yes, that's exactly what he used to do.' And they feel comforted and reassured that it really *is* their friend or husband or wife or whoever.

Sometimes, I can actually see the ghost of the person who has died standing beside the chair where their relative is sitting. Not always, but it often happens. Then I can describe them in much more detail.

You should not be afraid of ghosts. Unless you're visiting somewhere that is haunted for one particular reason, we usually only see ghosts because they *want* us to see them and, usually, that is because they loved us during their life and they love us still.

It is rare to be haunted by an evil spirit like the sailor in the farmhouse. Spirits usually don't make the effort to come through to you personally just to say, 'I didn't like you, I don't like you, I want to make your life a misery!'

So don't be afraid of ghosts. Don't actively seek them out but welcome them if they choose to appear.

I can understand the frustration of someone who is longing to see a ghost but never does. Yet it is more important that we all respect the spirits and wishes of those who have departed. In understanding that frustration I can understand, too, why people are tempted to use ouija boards to contact the other side, but I cannot say too strongly how dangerous these are.

You should never use a ouija board just as a bit of fun. You should never use them at all. Yes, you may very likely contact the other side, but you are not in control when you're using a ouija board. You cannot pick and choose the spirit you want to contact, you don't have the choice of a friendly or unfriendly spirit and you can accidently evoke evil spirits who will wish you nothing but harm.

It can all so easily go wrong and I know of one case in particular, when it did just that with devastating results.

When I was running my cleaning business there was a very nice young man who was sub-contracted by me to do all my glass. When I got a contract to clean a new house he did all the windows and things like that. Apart from my work he also had his own window-cleaning round and one day he was cleaning the windows of a little terraced house for an old lady and she invited him in for a cup of tea.

This old lady was fascinated by the spirit world and, while he was there working, she persuaded him to join her using the ouija board. She probably did not mean any harm, no doubt he thought it was a bit of a joke and they messed around with the board for quite a while.

The old lady's neighbour told me later that, suddenly, she saw this young man come tearing out of the house. He got into his van and screeched off, driving like a demon. That was not like him at all. He was a gentle man and always a careful driver.

He drove home, went into his garden shed, found an axe and tore into his house yelling he was going to kill his wife and children. Somebody sent for the police and it took six policemen to hold him down.

Not surprisingly, his family were distraught. They decided he had to be exorcised and called for a priest. During the exorcism the priest foolishly allowed the young man's sister to stay in the same room. She was young herself, young and vulnerable.

The boy's father watched what happened through the glass in the sitting room door. He swears that as the priest was performing the exorcism a foul black cloud came out of the young man's mouth, swirled around the priest and disappeared straight into the sister.

Since then the young man has been fine. But his sister, a lovely girl, changed. She became an alcoholic and nothing from that day to this has gone right for her, nothing.

While that evil spirit was entering the sister she probably had no idea what was happening. She would have felt nothing. I know because it has happened to me often although, thank God, never with such terrible results.

The first time it happened to me I was in my flat at Charlton, with my sister and a few other people, and I suddenly had this terrific feeling. I felt high, as if I'd taken some sort of drug. I couldn't rest. I was walking around the sitting room, up and down, up and down, pacing the floor. I knew something was happening to me but I wasn't sure what. I wasn't aware of anything but this amazing feeling of well-being. I was almost in a trance.

I stopped pacing and stood by the curtains and suddenly I heard my sister screaming. It woke me up and brought be back to eath with a jolt.

I said, 'What's happened?'

She said, 'You stood there, but it was as if you were in a ball of gold light!' It had frightened her, but for me it was an exciting experience. I was sure that just for that short time another spirit, a good spirit, had entered my body.

Since then it has happened to me frequently but it has never again been accompanied by that uplifting feeling of pleasure. In fact, I am usually completely unaware that anything out of the ordinary has taken place. I can only tell by the look on the face of the person who is with me and that is usually one of astonishment, because when they look at me they do not see me at all – they see the face of someone they have loved and lost.

I will be talking away to a client and suddenly they will cry out and say, 'Oh! You're my mother!' or 'my father!' They have seen their dead parent in me.

There is a name for this. It is transfiguration. What is happening is that the spirit of the dead person is so strong, and so keen to get through to the person who is with me, that they actually take over my body and my physical appearance. They literally transfigure me.

It can even happen with the spirit of someone who isn't dead. I know, because it happened while I was working on the case of Peter Sutcliffe, or the Yorkshire Ripper as we knew him then.

After months of senseless murders the police still had not caught him and one day I was sitting at home chatting to a reporter and a policewoman who was a friend of mine. I was getting very strong messages at that time about the Ripper's identity and I told the girls I would try to draw his face.

I had just taken up the pen, I was looking down at the paper and I could feel that sensation around my solar plexus which I always know means I'm on the right track. Suddenly, I looked up. Pamela, the policewoman, was white with shock. She got up from the chair and bolted out of the room.

Shirley, the reporter, was pale but she gripped the chair and didn't budge.

'Your face . . . it's changed. You're a man. You've got a beard.'

I wasn't aware of any change or movement in my facial muscles because I was so engrossed in getting into this man's mind. But they never forgot it. Of course, it was only later, after Sutcliffe had been arrested, that Shirley told me that his was the face she and Pamela had seen etched on my face. 'That face,' she said, 'that was you.'

And it happened again last year when I was interviewed by a lovely journalist called Angela Levin for the London-based Mail on Sunday magazine, *You*. Angela, it turned out, had arrived as a sceptic – but left with a much more open mind!

This is what she wrote about me:

'Nella came into the sitting room and when she saw me she did a double take. "Oh, it's you poppet," she said. "that's all right then. We've met before." I said that I didn't think we had.

"I don't mean in an ordinary way, lovey. Your face has flashed through my mind and I knew you'd be coming to see me." A shiver slid down my spine.

I glanced at her and when I did I froze in my shoes. For superimposed on her face was the face of my favourite uncle Issy Bonn who died 14 years ago. It wasn't that she looked like him. It was him or, at least, his smiling face. The image remained for several seconds. Then it disappeared. I have never felt more spooked.

I felt so baffled and overwhelmed that I wanted the experience to sink in before I decided whether or not to say anything about it. . . .'

In fact, Angela didn't say a word to me about it and, at the time, I felt nothing whatsoever. The first thing I knew about what had happened was when I read it in the magazine! But I hope, on reflection, Angela is pleased that she saw her uncle, Issy. He obviously loved her very much and merely took the opportunity to come and say hello.

One of the questions that Angela – and lots of other people for that matter – have asked me is why it is that Romany gypsies appear to be so much more psychic than other people. I told her I thought perhaps it was because we were more primitive than other peoples and I joked that maybe it was also because we didn't have much between our bloomin' ears!

But, seriously, I also think it's the way we Romanies are brought up. We are not taught to dismiss psychic phenomena as a load of old nonsense like many other people. We are brought up to accept the psychic world and to respect it.

When I was young and we were living in that caravan, and I cursed that woman who was having a go at Mum for lighting a fire and she fell off her horse, Mum didn't turn around to me and say, 'That was just coincidence.'

She was furious, and justifiably so, but only because she knew it *was not* a coincidence. She said, 'Don't do that again.' She acknowledged the power and I have always remembered that telling-off although if I have had to do it again it has always been with a very good cause.

There are no set words to a gypsy curse, none that I am aware of anyway, but I do know that a gypsy's curse usually works. Some people say that if you are wicked enough to put a curse on someone, the curse will rebound on you. I believe that is often true. But whether the curse comes back on you or not depends on the context in which it was made in the first place, and how justified you were in making that curse.

Never dismiss a gypsy's curse – no Romany would ever make a curse unless he or she was really angry. Too many people are terribly rude to gypsies. Why can't they be polite to gypsies and treat them like the human beings they are, instead of some lower form of life? Maybe they are wary of their power. In fact I have always believed that people generally exaggerate in their own minds the magical gifts of the Romany.

My mum never taught me how to make any secret potions or wonder cures. What she did teach me were what today's world would probably call 'old wives' tales', and that is exactly what they were. They go back for generations and generations, passed down from one wife to another. But there is nothing mysterious about most of them.

When I had the 'flu as a child I was given nothing more exotic than hot milk with a bit of rum in it – and, of course, camphorated oil on the chest; wonderful stuff that you can't buy any more. When I was older I was told that when I was a baby my two elder sisters were very ill with diphtheria. To cure them my father took the innards of an animal, burned them over the fire and then tied them around my sisters' feet to bring out the disease. It worked, too, and they both survived.

But most of the things I learned from my mother were the kind of household tips that have always been passed on from mother to daughter. The best one was how to wash clothes and clean cutlery. Even when we lived in the caravan, with the fire outside, my mother's washing was always spotless and shiny white and our cutlery sparkled.

The washing she did with an ordinary bar of soap and a washboard, but the secret of the cutlery was to clean the knives and forks with woodash from the fire and then rub them with a damp cloth. It worked a treat, and still does.

People probably don't like gypsies because they are frightened of them, just as many people do not like the idea of ghosts because it frightens them and they are unwilling to contemplate any paranormal phenomena because it opens up a vast field of new possibilities. Accept the paranormal and all the horizons and boundaries of your life change. And that, let's face it, is scary.

Fear is a terrible thing. Fear stops us all doing so much in our lives in one way or another. But if you can overcome fear of the unknown, and fear of what you don't understand, your life will be much richer.

I have often said that my gift is not a blessing but a curse. Sometimes, because of my gift, I have to go through experiences, or come into contact with feelings and events, that I would much rather avoid: the evil of a murderer's mind, the despair of a mother whose child is lost, the hopelessness of a cancer victim. I can never say no if someone asks for help and I work so hard that I am constantly tired and suffer every day with terrible headaches. In fact I don't know of one psychic whose health hasn't suffered in some way from their work.

But, I also find the spirits I come into contact with a great comfort and, as I get older, a great source of pleasure too.

Last year I was feeling very low for personal reasons and once again my health was poorly. One day I decided to buy a piano, not for me, but for my grandchildren. They often pop round to my house and I thought it would be good for them to make music in their lives.

I had never owned a piano before. We were too poor when I was a child and later, when I had grown up, the money always had to go on essentials.

I can't read music and the only tune I can play is 'Three Blind Mice' with one finger. That is the sum of my musical talent! Until last year, that is . . .

The piano had been sitting in my sitting room for abuut five months. The kids weren't that interested in it. After the initial novelty had worn off they hardly played at all so most of the time it just sat there silently.

One Autumn evening a friend of mine called Lou droppd in for a cup of tea. We had our cup of tea and I thought I would just take the cups into the kitchen to wash up. I came away from the kitchen sink and I said, 'Lou, I've got to sit at the piano.'

'What for? You can't play.'

'I know that. But I know I've got to sit at the piano.'

He knows me quite well and he must have seen some change in my face, or some look about me, that made him think, 'There's something going on here.'

I sat down at the piano while he dashed out and grabbed the radio-cassette recorder from the kitchen.

And then it happened. I sat there and I was playing the piano like a professional and the music just came and I felt wonderful. It wasn't modern music, or music hall music, it was timeless music, almost the kind you would hear in church or at a classical concert. The tunes flowed on and on. After an hour my fingers stopped. I could hardly believe this wonderful new gift I had been given. The sense of accomplishment was enormous and I was afraid the whole experience was a one-off. But the next day I sat at the piano and it happened again. And the next, and the next.

I have been able to play the piano ever since, although I still can't read music and I don't know what it is I'm playing. While it's happening I feel as if these are my hands moving over the keys but at the same time they are not my hands. So, I don't think about my hands at all. I just let my fingers go where they want to go and let the music come.

The music is very sweet, I think that is the best way to describe it. It is very emotional. Now I often play during my healing sessions and it makes people want to cry. Nobody says a word, all they want to do is sit and listen to this music. It does something to them, and for them.

Sometimes the music sounds familiar but, just when you're beginning to think you know the tune, it flows into something completely different. When my brother first heard me play last year, I finished the piece and looked at him and there were tears streaming down his face.

'But you can't play,' he said.

'I know I couldn't, but I can now.'

I don't understand the music myself but it seems to come to me when I am feeling particularly low or under pressure. And now the same is happening with poetry. I used to write poetry as a teenager – the sort most teenage girls do – full of romance and dreams of love. Very flowery stuff!

Since then, I haven't had much time to write but, at about the same time as I started to play the piano, I also felt compelled to put pen to paper. I began one Autumn evening. All day I had been inundated with people, the phone never stopped ringing and clients were turning up on the doorstep every five minutes. There had been so many people in distress saying, 'Help me, Nella,' so many tears, and I wasn't feeling too bright myself.

That night, as usual, I said my prayers. But I was not thanking God. I felt angry and sick to my soul. I spoke aloud, 'God, who do you think I am? What am I, a doormat? Who am I?' By now I was shouting, 'Who am I?'

Then suddenly I heard the voice of a spirit.

He said, 'Do you want to know who you are?'

'Yes, I do.'

'So,' he said, 'take out your pen.'

I took out my pen and then he said, 'Write this . . .'

And that is how I came to write this poem:

> I'm the friend to a lonely stranger.
> I'm the mother that calms your fears.
> I'm the mistress to the businessman.
> I'm the nurse that can dry your tears.
>
> I'm the sister to the brother.
> I'm the wife of a happy man.
> Whatever you want in a woman
> That is what I am.

I have been writing poems regularly ever since. First of all the feelings come – and I only write about things I feel very deeply about – then the words flow. Often I am crying while I am writing them, they are so strong and powerful.

I believe this is the spirits' way of letting me release all the emotion that is stored up in me. I am just one big bundle of emotions. All psychics are. But with the music and the poems I am being given an outlet.

Before I write, or before I play the piano, I have to have the urge, a certain feeling. If I don't have that feeling it doesn't work. I have tried to play the piano just to show people what I can do but, if I don't have the feeling, it doesn't work. I sit there and I cannot play a thing, it's back to 'Three Blind Mice' again! But, once I get the feeling, I'm off. It usually happens when I'm feeling a bit lost and lonely.

I do not understand what happens myself, but the music and the poems are both a great comfort to me. I do believe that artists, musicians and writers who have passed on to the other side can come back and help others to paint or play musical instruments or write.

So, maybe it is a spirit who, in their earthly life, enjoyed playing the piano and writing poetry who is now coming back to help me with the words and music. I don't know.

If it is a returning spirit they are doing it for a reason: they may be gaining pleasure for themselves and they are certainly giving pleasure to me. But perhaps, they feel their life's work was not finished and once completed through me, they will go away again.

I can understand that. But there are many strange talents in the psychic world that I see no purpose in at all. Levitation is one. When I first saw my monk at Bexley Abbey I felt as if I was raised in the air, that my feet actually left the ground, but maybe it was merely that I felt spiritually lifted.

To me, whether I was actually suspended above the earth or not is irrelevant. Perhaps I was, perhaps I wasn't. I believe that all things are possible but I have to admit to being baffled by the purpose of some psychic phenomena or, at least, by how it is used by some people.

I have no doubt that some psychics can levitate people to order for an audience. But what's the point? God gave me two good legs to walk on so why do I need to levitate? I really can't see the sense in using all that psychic energy merely to lift someone from the floor.

I admire Uri Geller, and I am sure he's an excellent psychic with an exceptional mind. But why spend all that time and energy bending spoons?

I totally accept that he can bend spoons merely with the power of his mind. The mind is a fantastic organ, doctors can cut pieces out of the human brain but even the greatest medical experts on the planet cannot fully explain the workings of the human mind. So, I am sure Uri Geller can do what he says he can do. But what is the purpose in bending spoons except, perhaps, to show that you can bend spoons?

I believe that the gifts we have all been given should not be used in the pursuit of fame and fortune alone. We should be using them to benefit humanity and to make the world a better place to live in, not so much for ourselves but for those who will come after us.

Sadly, there will always be people who use their psychic power for evil rather than for good and, what is worse, it is a growing trend. People think there is much more excitement in being wicked than in being good. Look where being good has got me – bad health, alone and stony broke most of the time. But, still, I think I will stay sick, I will stay broke and I will stay on the right path.

God gave Man free will and all of us can use whatever power we have for good or for evil. On the other side there are evil spirits just as there are good ones, and those who have a strong psychic power can, I believe, call up those evil spirits.

There is a horrifying amount of black magic, and even voodoo, still being practised in this country and all over the world; so much so that if the average person were to know how widespread it was it would throw them into a complete state of panic.

I know this is true. I can feel it. And many people have come to see me who have been victims of black magic or who have had voodoo spells put on them.

Counteracting the effects of black magic is a form of healing – not healing of physical ill health, but spiritual healing in the truest sense of the word. To heal someone who has been the victim of black magic you must use stronger white magic to combat it.

White magic consists of age old secrets that I do not believe should be revealed too openly and I don't intend to do so here, except to say that they are based on prayer and purity.

A lot of people dismiss black magic as hocus-pocus and sheer bunkum, but if you saw the effects it can have on a person you would not say that. Black magic can destroy a person and pain their soul intolerably.

I remember one woman who came to see me who had been the victim of a voodoo spell. She was a Nigerian lady, married to an accountant who had been coming to see me for clairvoyance, and after a couple of visits he suggested shyly that I might be able to help his wife.

His wife, he said, couldn't see. She had visited eye specialists and been to hospital time and time again but, still, they could not find anything wrong with her eyes. In fact, her eyes looked perfect but her vision was completely blurred. Apart from disturbing her everyday life she was upset that her illness had started just as she was planning to take her driving test.

As soon as she walked into my front room I knew she was having voodoo directed at her. I could sense it. I also knew that before I could heal her, before I could even touch her, I had to prepare myself. I had to be clean and pure and I left her and her husband while I went to the bathroom and literally scrubbed my body from top to bottom so I was physically thoroughly cleansed.

Friends often comment on how sparkling clean my house usually is. I am houseproud, always have been and that's the way I was brought up, but that is not the only reason for the cleanliness. To do the healing work I do, I must work in a clean environment.

After I had scrubbed myself I put on a clean white nightdress and came back into the room. I put my hands over her eyes and, when I did, I could feel a kind of sticky rope coiled up in them, that is the only way to describe it. I started to gently pull on this rope and, as I did, she was crying out in pain, 'Oh my eyes, my eyes.'

In fact, by now, I wasn't touching her at all. My hands hovered inches away from her and I felt I was pulling on this rope, pulling, pulling, pulling until I had it all out. When I had done that she looked at me in astonishment. Her eyes had cleared – she could see. And, incidentally, she went on to pass her driving test!

Unless you have ever had evil directed at you, and specifically you, you cannot imagine how awful it is and how badly it can affect you. Yet there are so many sayings about the experience which we take totally for granted. We say, 'God pays his debts without money' or 'He who does evil will have evil done unto him.' And we use the expression 'to wish him ill'. It is not myth or fancy, I honestly believe you *can* wish someone ill.

Often, even though people deny the paranormal and deny psychic power within themselves, they will still, nevertheless, have some uncanny feeling, some kind of hunch that something in life is working against them beyond their control. Do not ignore those hunches. Of course, it may be just a hunch – but it may be something more. Much more.

It is difficult when you get feelings like this to confide in anyone. You are naturally afraid that your friends will think you are silly. But my advice is to trust your instincts, and there are things you can do to counteract any evil influences that are being directed towards you.

A friend told me this story. Her daughter was married to a man she strongly believed to be involved in some kind of witchcraft or black magic. She disapproved of him and of how he was running her daughter's life and eventually she didn't bother to hide that disapproval. She went to stay with them and that night her son-in-law and a male friend said they wouldn't be retiring to bed that night because they had to stay up and 'work'.

During the night she had terrible nightmares – nightmares she described as waking nightmares. They were nightmares, but she was sure she was awake. She felt a great darkness descending on her and when she looked up there were three swords which looked as if they were suspended from the ceiling and about to stab her. She spent a sleepless night.

It is an odd story but I am sure the man and his friend were summoning up what psychic energy they could muster to intimidate this woman and to frighten her.

In this situation prayer is your best defence. Even people who don't believe in God subconsciously have a belief in good and find themselves praying in times of crisis. 'Someone help me . . .'

In a situation like this, use the Lord's Prayer. Even if you are not a Christian, the familiarity of it, the ritual of it, will help. But if what is happening to you is not an isolated incident, and you feel you are continuously being bombarded with evil intentions, then perhaps it is best to seek out someone like me, or a reputable member of the spiritualist church, who will be able to heal you spiritually.

It should be someone who knows what they're doing but I honestly don't believe it matters what faith they belong to. What you have to look for is a good soul, a genuinely good soul. They will not turn you away and the greatest enemy of evil is a good soul.

SEVEN

A Glimpse
into the Next Room

'Death is nothing at all . . . I have simply slipped away into the next room . . . I am I and you are you . . . Whatever we were to each other, that we are still. Call me by my old familiar name, speak to me in the easy way which you always used. Put no difference in your tone; wear no false air of solemnity or sorrow. Laugh as we always laughed at the little jokes we enjoyed together. Play, smile, think of me, pray for me. Let my name be ever the household word that it always was. Let it be spoken without an effort, without the ghost of a shadow on it. Life means all that it ever meant. It is the same as it ever was; there is absolutely unbroken continuity. What is death but a negligible accident? Why should I be out of mind because I am out of sight? I am but waiting for you for an interval, somewhere very near, just around the corner. All is well.'

CANON SCOTT-HOLLAND,
1847–1918

Death. It is the final and inevitable equaliser and most people, at least in the Western World, spend much of their lives in fear of it. In the East it is a different story, because their faith in an afterlife has convinced them that, when we die, we do not simply disappear off the face of the Earth forever; we go on to something better. In many countries, they do not dress in black to mourn the dead. Instead, they celebrate the death, because they know that this person is now just one more step up on the ladder to Nirvana, perfection, God.

I believe that dying can be a beautiful experience. Dying is the easy part. Living here in this life, that's the hard part.

I am one hundred per cent sure that death is not the end. There is no such thing as death; it is merely a transition from one state to another. When we die, our souls do not die with us. Dying is simply living in a different dimension. When we die, we merely pass into the next room and we still have the power to contact those who are living in this room, in this world.

I am sure that one of the reasons spirits contact me from the other side is to explain to me, and to give proof to the people I am with, that there really is an afterlife.

The transition we go through in death is similar to the one we go through at birth. We start as an embryo, all nice and cosy in mummy's womb for nine months and then there is the transition into this great big world where we breathe our own air, and fulfil our own destiny. At the end of our life span we go through another transition.

We are all physical beings, made of flesh and bones and blood, but I want you to imagine that we are also spiritual people; we have a soul. If you can, imagine the shape of your spiritual body housed inside your physical body. That's your soul, you spirit.

Now, you can chop off my leg, my physical leg, but you can't chop off my spiritual leg. Many people who have had a limb amputated by surgery, swear afterwards that they can still feel that limb. Of course they can, because their spiritual leg is still there. You cannot destroy it, and it is the same with death. The body can actually die but you cannot destroy the spirit. How do you chop up a spirit? The answer is you can't.

I have been with many people when they have died and sometimes I have been lucky enough actually to see the spirit leave the body. Often a light appears and you can see it come from the body, rise up and disappear.

Sometimes the spirit will leave the body before the person has actually been pronounced dead by the doctors.

The person may be lying there unconscious, or in a coma, and the spirit knows that the body is no longer needed, so it leaves it. That's why it is quite common to hear people claiming to have 'seen' Uncle George, or whoever, at eight o'clock in the evening when he wasn't pronounced dead until five or ten minutes past. His spirit left his body before the moment of physical death.

Many people, who have 'died' on the operating table and then been resuscitated, have reported out-of-the-body experiences. They die and they look down on themselves, because their soul has briefly left their physical body. In spirit they think it is time to leave that body and move on, but then the body is brought back, the physical life is resuscitated and they realise the spirit is needed back in that body. It is not yet time to go.

Sometimes I believe other spirits send them back, tell them it is not their time and that they have got some more living to do in this world.

I have never been in that situation, thank God, but no one who has ever been through it has described it as frightening or even unpleasant. On the contrary, most of them have said they felt at peace and that the experience cured them of their fear of death.

So what will happen to me, or to you, when we die?

A lot of people who have died, and then come back, say they experienced going through a dark tunnel. I believe that is what happens. Our spirit leaves our body and as it travels through a kind of tunnel we experience the transition of leaving the physical world behind and entering the spirit world which is, after all, only another dimension.

Often we are met by people we have loved in this life. Grandparents, parents, husbands or wives come to greet us and to be reunited. Sometimes, especially when it is a child who has died in a tragic accident, the spirit of a family member will actually come to the child's body and escort their spirit to the other side.

What you leave behind is an empty shell. Many, many people who lose a loved one choose to visit them for a final goodbye in the undertakers or Chapel of Rest and, almost without exception, anyone who has done this will tell you that they feel that the person has somehow 'gone', that the person they loved is no more.

Even if they do not understand the feeling, even if they do not believe in an afterlife, they are aware that the body is now just flesh and they are conscious of the spiritual loss. And, of course, they are right because, by then, the spirit is long gone and settled in a happier place.

Once over the other side your friends and family welcome you and make you feel at home. Many people have challenged me saying, 'If you can contact the people on the other side and they can contact you, why don't they talk about what it's like over there?'

And I always reply, 'But they do!' From what they have told me, and people like me, it is very beautiful over there on the other side. If you went over for a brief glimpse you would think it was just another place in our world. There is a real life over there. There are spirits of all ages, there are schools, there are hospitals. But, of course, they are nothing like those we have here.

For example, little children can play in the water and not get wet.

They can fall over and not hurt themselves. And just imagine it, suppose you and I were over there right now and we fancied some caviar we would have the taste of that caviar – without the caviar.

We wouldn't be physically eating it but we would think we were. We wouldn't go through the physical motions of eating the caviar but we would feel all the pleasures associated with it.

Or, say we wanted to sit by a cosy log fire on a winter's night, we could experience that and feel the warmth and pleasure whenever we wanted to.

Whatever you want, it is there, because the whole of your life is built up of memories and emotions. That is all life is. You are building memories every day and your experience of living is one never-ending jumble of emotions.

Every day you are experiencing physical actions and reactions, from something as simple as breathing to something as basic as making love. But most of your living, the most important part of your living, is really just based on emotion.

Imagine everything you have gone through in life; bring different memories into your mind. Do they all conjure up different feelings? Now imagine the sensations of those feelings without the physical 'edge' – that is what it is like on the other side in the spirit world.

People often chide me, saying that if the other side is much like this one, then the afterlife will be even more complicated and problematical than life on this side ever was! For example, one question I am forever being asked is, 'What if, in this life, you've had two lovers or two husbands and now all three of you are dead and you're all on the other side. What happens then?'

But a situation like that is no problem at all. You must expand your mind and try to understand life in another dimension. You see, in the spirit world if you had loved both those men you don't split up, you are all together. There is no feeling of jealousy or animosity; that is gone. There will be just three souls, three spirits, and the genuine love you gave out while you were in this world, and which has carried over with you.

People are often surprised when I say that there are hospitals on the other side. Of course they are not like the hospitals we have here which look after our physical bodies. These are spiritual hospitals; they look after our spirit.

I cannot think of a better word for them. They are quiet places where people who have had tragic lives and deaths can go to be healed. There they meet lovely spirits who calm them, and comfort them through the transition; spirits who explain, 'You're in the spirit world now and you can rest here with us. We're going to look after you until you fully realise that you are living in another dimension.'

'Look, your loved ones are still alive over there and they are quite safe. You can see them and, once you're strong enough, you can go and visit them at any time.'

I do not believe there are towns, as such, on the other side but I do think there are buildings in some form. I remember once, when I was praying, I had a vision. I saw a beautiful place from a distance, then suddenly I was visiting this place, I was in the vision and I was in a building. It wasn't a dream, I wasn't on the Earth, I was given a glimpse of somewhere else.

I do not know where the building was; I can only say I felt as though it was 'up'. That may not make sense to you but it is the only way I can find to describe how it felt.

There was a big, wide, long corridor with lovely arches. Someone said, 'Nella, go down to the end.' I walked down to the end and found myself looking over the edge of a balcony. I was almost as high as the mountains I could see in the distance. It was a fantastic view – hazy, but very beautiful.

And all I could think of when I came out of this vision was something I had read in the Bible. 'In my Father's house there are many mansions.' And I immediately thought, 'That is one of the mansions the Good Book was talking about.' It was wonderful.

Was it a dream? I don't know. Maybe I was lucky enough to be allowed a glimpse, just a fleeting glimpse, into the next room.

Once you transfer from this plane of life to another, you will be able to say to yourself: 'I was alive a little while ago and now I'm alive in a different dimension and I have no fear any more. In this dimension I will understand so much more, and I will see into my soul.'

On the other side I believe we can find peace. All the beauty we see on this side is also on the other side. And there is even more beauty of a different kind. Say, for example, you have been disabled in this life; over there it will be gone. Over there you can move freely. There is no physical pain.

And, most of important of all, you will have no fear of death – for you have been through what people call death and have survived it. Of everything on Earth most people fear, they fear death the most. But once you have passed through that barrier the fear cannot hurt you or cloud your judgement and actions. Nothing can physically hurt you because you are already dead and that, more than anything else, changes your entire outlook and perspective.

I do not believe we change our basic personalities, the very essence of us, when we go over to the other side, but we do change the way we look at things. We can look back and see clearly what we did with our lives.

I have met many spirits who are full of remorse for their earthly life and who really want to make amends. They apologise and say, 'Now I can see what I did wrong and I am truly sorry. I'm trying to make amends from this side,' and they can do it. Often they will ask me to apologise to a loved one for something they did which they now see as cruel and inconsiderate.

Once you are on the other side, you can see all the mistakes you made, where you went wrong and whether you did things out of greed or malice. You can be more honest with yourself. You have to be, once you are over there; your soul has no hiding place from the truth.

You become wiser after death because you no longer have the restriction of only being able to see what is around you. You are not confined to the senses of physical feeling and touch. You can look back at your earthly life then, because time there doesn't exist. You can see yesterday, today, tomorrow – they are all one.

The whole pattern suddenly becomes clear.

What is time? No one can tell you because time does not exist. Once your spirit is free of your physical body you can appreciate so much more. There are limited things you can do inside a physical body but, take that away, and the possibilities are endless.

Time, one of man's inventions, no longer matters. That is why I can see things that have not happened yet but are going to happen some time in the future. By some stange quirk there is something in my mind that enables me to see the whole concept; to see the entire pattern of someone's life. On the other side we can all do that.

There have been many stories of people who have somehow stepped back or stepped forward in time and I am sure that it is quite possible. I belive it is the key to the secret of the famous Bermuda Triangle in the Atlantic, where so many ships and aeroplanes have apparently disappeared into thin air.

They haven't disappeared at all. All that they have done is accidentally found the door to another time, another dimension. And sometimes, years later, some of them are able to find the door out again. Many more don't find the way back and continue living in the other dimension.

One story of time travel particularly sticks in my mind. I was appearing on a TV show about the paranormal and three young men were also guests. Their story was quite remarkable, although the young men themselves weren't remarkable at all, they were very ordinary, very pleasant and I am sure they were absolutely genuine.

They told of how they were all on holiday camping somewhere in the English countryside. One night they were walking home from a pub and they took a short cut down a lane, over a stile and through some fields.

It was late at night, there was a full moon and, as they approached the next field, they could hear the voices of lots of people, the sound of animals and children laughing.

They walked on and suddenly it was daylight and they found themselves in a Saxon village. There were children playing, animals in pens, men at work, women cooking and chatting. They described it as being like stepping into a film set of Saxon times.

No one took any notice of them. Then, as they stepped back, the village disappeared. They stepped forward again, and there it was; back and it was gone.

No doubt the sceptics will say they should not have stayed so long in the pub! But I believe they accidentally stepped through the door into another dimension. When they were questioned afterwards, they all saw the same things and I, for one, believe them because it has happened to me.

I remember once I was lying in bed in that state when you're half awake and half asleep.

Suddenly I was dreaming – but was I dreaming? I felt wide awake and I was walking along a road. The road was made of cobbles, but not the round cobbles you find in old English villages. These were square cobbles, like an early form of paving stone.

There was no pavement but there were houses on both sides of the road, rather like Church Cottages in Eynsford where you opened the front door and walked straight into the sitting room.

I knew that I lived in one of these houses and I lived in this place. I was walking towards a market and I was holding the hand of a child who was walking beside me. He was about seven or eight and I knew he was my child.

We reached the market and I was shopping for Christmas, but what was on sale wasn't anything like most of the treats we buy these days for the Christmas holiday. There were gingerbread shapes on sale, different kinds of home-made biscuits and colourful candies, all obviously home made.

We walked on and they were selling lovely vegetables from stalls and there were chickens in crates and other animals. I knew that I was married and my husband worked in an office as a clerk. These days, that may not be thought of as special, but I was proud of it. Being a clerk was a job of high status in those days and I felt privileged. It wasn't an easy life but it was far better than many other people were living at that time.

I was still awake, but then the picture faded around me and I was back at home, in our time. I was in a state of shock. I thought, 'That was *me* walking down the street, and that was *me* with *my* child, that was *me* in a previous life.

I thought about the experience many times afterwards. I do not know when or where the village was but I think the time was back in the 18th Century and I am fairly certain it was England. It wasn't an unpleasant experience but it was strange and it stayed with me for days afterwards.

Far more frightening was something that happened here in good old, ordinary Bexleyheath High Street and, again, I think I somehow stepped through to another dimension.

The day started ordinarily enough. I picked up my shopping bag and walked down the High Street to buy some bread from the lovely baker's down the road.

I went into the baker's and suddenly, inside the shop, my surroundings started to change and distort. It was scary. I managed somehow to stumble out of the shop; I don't know what they must have thought of me. Once outside I looked around and thought, 'Where am I? This isn't Bexleyheath, at least not the Bexleyheath I know.'

I could hear my own footsteps but there was no other sound. There were no other people, no traffic, nothing. I seemed to be alone in this strange place. The buildings had changed. The supermarket had gone, the bank, all the sights I'm so used to.

Now the buildings were made of marble. They were not very tall, their windows were tiny and I couldn't see any doors. I remember thinking, 'Oh God, where's Lion Road?' which is just around the corner from my house.

There were no other people; the silence was deafening and I was very frightened. I kept thinking, 'I must find my way back.' I was still wearing the same clothes; I was still holding my carrier bag, with the loaf of bread I'd bought in it, but I did not know this place.

I don't know how long I walked up and down this street. It felt like a long time. Then I got to where the baker's shop used to be and as I walked past his shop, suddenly, it was all there again in front of me, the Bexleyheath I knew. There were the people and the traffic and the buildings. It was comforting but I felt terribly shaken and got home as soon as possible. I was physically ill for three weeks after that.

I could not get the experience out of my mind. It was as if I had stepped through a time barrier. I don't know how long I was gone. At the time it felt like an age, but maybe it was just a few minutes or even seconds. I do know that I left our time for a while and then came back to exactly the same place.

I do not pretend to understand what happened and I do not know why it happened. But I don't dismiss it. I am well aware that people might say I had simply gone mad for a while but I am sure there is more to it than that. I stumbled onto, or into, another dimension.

There are so many channels, so many facets to this life. Life is like a diamond with a million sides to it. You can start to travel somewhere and arrive in a totally different place to the one you set out for.

I think many people get flashes of an earlier life; I am a great believer in reincarnation.

I believe in God. On the other side we are closer to God. We may not see Him but we can feel Him. I feel God here but it will be much stronger on the other side. I am religious but I cannot believe in a Heaven and a Hell because I'm sure we all go to the same place.

I also believe in Darwin's Theory of Evolution. So, how can I reconcile all these beliefs which many might say are contradictory? Easily – for, to me, it is the most logical explanation of life.

I believe there is a ladder of life as Darwin said – although obviously I won't explain it nearly as well as he did! I believe it starts with light which then grows into the most primitive forms of life. As that light and life die it is reincarnated, a little further up the ladder, in a more sophisticated form of life.

You cannot progress backwards – that is a basic contradiction. Once you have lived one life, you live the next, on and on through the chain and up the ladder. Of course, we are descended from apes. But, finally, the ape is reincarnated as a human. Once you live life as a human you cannot be reincarnated as an ape or an ant.

The next time you will be reincarnated as another human – but, hopefully, as one who has learned from his or her previous life. And in the next life you will learn the lessons you failed to learn in your previouis lives.

As, spiritually, you become better through your lives, you understand more; you are more at peace and so you reach higher dimensions and higher planes until eventually, hopefully, you reach what the Eastern religions call Nirvana, perfection and bliss, but which I call, simply, God.

Before you can be reincarnated you have to come to terms with your previous life as you have lived it. You must accept both the good and the bad you have instigated. You have to make some recompense for the bad. It's up to God, and God alone, how you do that.

I believe that some spirits on the other side may be left in limbo for a long time until they can honestly see where they strayed from the right path. Maybe they are even set apart to consider their previous life before they join the other spirits. I think that many who go over to the other side have still to get rid of their earthly arrogance. For a time they continue to try to justify their earthly mistakes, even though they may have behaved in a shameful way. It takes time before they gradually 'see the light'.

Many people cannot accept that they are dead, especially if their death has been sudden. They don't want to believe that they have left the earthly dimension and moved on to the next. Some can be quite angry that their life has been cut short. I know, because they tell me so. They say, 'Why me? It's not fair!' They are still preoccupied with their former life. But they move on in the end. I think we all do, although, God knows, it is hard work.

I am not of the school of thought that believes that, because someone has passed to the other side, they immediately become some kind of angel, all sweetness and light, unselfish and working only for the good.

I have been contacted by malevolent spirits, spirits who haven't learned, who still feel bitterness. But, on the other side, they are eventually forced to come to terms with those feelings.

When a person is murdered, for example, they often feel resentful when they get to the other side, hurt that their life has been snatched away from them. Maybe some of them, higher up the spiritual ladder, can forgive and say, 'He or she didn't know what they were doing. They haven't yet reached a higher plane, they are a lesser mortal, they have a lot to learn and I forgive them.'

But others, I am sure, return in spirit to their murderers. They have not forgiven and they quite literally come back to haunt their killer. Then you find that the guilty man or woman suffers from terrible nightmares or turns to drink or to drugs to help themselves forget what they have done. They are haunted and afraid because they feel the person they have killed is there at their shoulder. And they are quite right. He is.

It is all very sad. But I think in the majority of cases, if someone has lived a bad life, a life in which they have shown little respect for other souls and from which they have learned nothing, they do learn something in the spirit world.

On the other side, they not only look back and see what they did, they can also see all the consequences of their actions. It is so true that 'no man is an island'; we are all part of God's whole and whatever we do affects other people. Even the silliest everyday decisions we make invariably have an effect on somebody else.

These people can suddenly see the havoc, the misery and heartache they caused in life and it is a very poor spirit who isn't moved to feel remorse. But I believe that many of us have guides who see us through life, who are there to help, just like the old man I call Father.

They are not the spirits of people we know in our earthly life but somehow they adopt us. They want to make amends for wrong-doings in their own previous life by guiding us so that we do not make the same mistakes as they did.

People who have behaved despicably in this life, hurting many people, are not the only ones whose spirits are badly troubled when they pass from this world into the next.

It is a common idea that the spirits of people who commit suicide are doomed never to find peace, but to wander aimlessly and unhappily on this earth, somehow suspended between one world and the next.

I really do not believe that is true at all. Anyone who is driven to the ultimate edge, to commit suicide, is in a terrible state of mind, and when you pass over to the other side I believe you take your state of mind with you. It does not instantly change and, sometimes, it takes a long while before you will find peace in your soul.

That doesn't mean that the souls of people who have killed themselves are permanently earthbound. I think they do have a harder time of it. They go before their time, so the spirits on the other side, who would normally be there to meet and guide them, are absent. That means the victim of suicide has to make that momentous journey, the transition to the next world, alone. It is much more difficult, but they do it.

Once there, I'm sure they are looked after and cared for until they can come to terms with what has happened and return to spiritual health. Although that, I think, could take a long time.

I believe that as spirits we ourselves choose when and how we are reincarnated. So why don't we all come back as rich, beautiful, adored and successful? Unfortunately it doesn't work like that! We can only be reincarnated when we have learned from our past mistakes and can see what we have to learn in the next life. And, as often as not, we know the lessons have to be painful.

Most children who die or are killed, and pass over to the other side at a young earthly age, grow up in the spirit world – unless they choose to be quickly reincarnated. Children can be reincarnated sooner than many adults because there is no sin in a child. The more sin, the more time it takes you to assess and learn from your previous life and the longer it is before you are reincarnated.

We all choose to be reincarnated for a reason. Once you are a spirit it is not a question of what you want or what would be most comfortable: it is a question of what is necessary.

Once the decision has been taken and the choice of life has been made, that speck of life that is your soul returns to this earthly dimension at the very moment of conception.

During your new life you may very well have no recollection at all of your previous lives, or of the spirit world, although it is all there for you to see if you will only use your psychic eye.

One of the great inponderables of reincarnation is: 'Do we meet the same people?'

When a man says to a woman, 'We were meant for each other,' or, 'We were destined to be together?' is that just a case of the relationship in a previous life not having reached its right conclusion or fulfilment?

I believe that in this life we do meet people we have known in a previous life – not just one person, but whole groups of people. I believe that almost all the people you know and love – or know and don't even particularly like – you knew in the last life and will probably meet in the next.

I think the link between loved ones is particularly strong. Maybe in your last life your daughter was in fact your mother, maybe she was your brother, but there is an unbreakable link there and from every relationship there is a lot to learn.

Once on the other side you can see things clearly. 'I got that wrong and that wrong.' Our aim, as souls, is to get better and better so when we come back in another life we go through that relationship again and, probably, again and again. But each time we look at it from a different perspective and, hopefully, as we progress, we begin to get it right. The things we did wrong in a relationship last time we get right next time, things that we left undone we finish.

Does that mean that if there is someone in this life we detest that we will meet them in the next?

Yes, I think so. But hopefully we are wiser. What we will do this time is sit down and say to ourselves: why? What is it about this person that I dislike so much? More often than not we will come to the unpleasant conclusion that maybe what we don't like about them is a reflection of the bad qualities we see in ourselves, the weaknesses we'd rather not think about. You recognise something you don't like about yourself in that person and you think: 'I don't like that.'

If you did behave badly in your previous life, if there are specific lessons for you to learn – and usually there are – then there will be some memory of what you have to do to make amends.

Very subtly you will be conscious of it. You will prepare to do something and a feeling deep within you will tell you that it is wrong: that this is something you did before and it was as wrong then as it is now.

No doubt you won't call it a memory of an earlier life or a mistake. You will simply call it your conscience.

You chose the path of your life on this earth, you chose it before you came back. I know that many hypnotists claim to be able to regress people to their former lives and I don't doubt for a minute that they can. But what's the point?

Whatever it was, whoever it was, has gone. I am here to learn new lessons and I hope I am doing that properly. I chose to come back as I am, therefore I must have known that it was going to be a damned hard road.

I must have known that in the beginning but I thought, 'That's the life that I need, I can tackle that, I'll take that . . .' Most babies, I believe, are born old souls.

People often ask me about animals on the other side. Of course there are animals there! They are there waiting to move on like the rest of us. And I do believe that animals come back to visit loved ones on this side. I know it because I've seen them.

When I am giving a reading to someone who has just lost a husband or wife, the person who has died will often come back bringing a dog or a cat, in spirit, with them.

Sometimes the first thing I have said to someone is, 'This man is here and he's with a little brown and white dog.'

And the wife will say, 'That's our dog. He passed over a couple of months before John did. But they were always very close.' And I can say in all honesty, 'Well, now they're together again.'

Sometimes I can be giving someone a reading and a cat or dog will appear in spirit and start nuzzling the person's legs. You can even see the owners instinctively reach down to stroke their dead pet. Once again, it's the love-link. Love lives on. You can't kill love. Whatever you do to someone, whatever is done unto you, you can't kill love.

I know I'm privileged to get glimpses of the other side. Lord only knows why I can and others can't. But maybe you will, if you open your mind and your heart just a little more. It will come to you slowly, in flashes, but once you learn to trust what you see with your psychic eye, a new world will open up to you and you will learn so much.

I don't think for a minute that I must be high up the spiritual ladder because I am allowed to see some of those from the other side who come and visit us from time to time.

Someone like Mother Teresa must be very high up the scale and well on her way to God. But the likes of you and I have a very long, long way to go yet. We can only do our best. And maybe humility, accepting that we have much to learn, will help us to get there.

I know it is a cliché, but I am very conscious in this life that I mustn't hurt other people and I don't think I have ever knowingly or deliberately hurt anyone. It is almost impossible to live a life without hurting one of your fellow human beings but I have never gone out of my way to do so.

And I have never turned my back on anyone who needed help. Sometimes I wish I didn't have the gift to help people, but I do. It is God's gift, and so I must use it.

Now that I am nearer to the end of my life than to the beginning, I can see that helping and healing people is the purpose of my life – this time.

I honestly do not fear death. Like everyone else I fear pain and I would not want a painful death. But physical pain can be eased by drugs and they are discovering more effective pain-killing drugs all the time.

If it was part of the pattern that I had to die now I would not be afraid to go to the other side. In fact I would find it fascinating, since I have spent so much of this life in a kind of twilight world between the two – contacted by one side, and considered a bit of a crank because of it, by the other.

But I would be sad that I haven't done all the things in this life that I would like to do. I love painting and I would like to have time to paint; I would love to create a beautiful garden; I'd love to travel and see different peoples and cultures.

Due to my work, I haven't had a lot of time in this life to myself because much of it has been spent in contact with the other side, for other people. Ironic, isn't it?

EIGHT

My right to reply

'No paranormal, psychic or supernatural claim has ever been substantiated by proper testing. I'm very familiar with how people are deceived by tricks and how they deceive themselves.'

JAMES RANDI, MAGICIAN
THE SUNDAY PEOPLE, 1991

Question:
'Does visiting a psychic or spiritualist matter? If it makes people happy, if it reassures them, if it makes them feel comfortable, then does it matter?'

ROBERT KILROY-SILK, PRESENTER,
SPEAKING ON HIS TV SHOW *KILROY*.

'I think truth does matter. I think visiting a psychic or spiritualist does harm people psychologically but it's also the mere fact that it's conning people. It's conning them in this pretence that they can be in touch with dead people and it's also conning them out of money.'

BARBARA SMOKER,
PRESIDENT OF THE NATIONAL SECULAR SOCIETY.
BBC TV, JANUARY 1992

Not so very long ago – a matter of a mere few hundred years – I would have been burned at the stake. As it is I'm quite used to being called a crank and a witch. In fact where I live in Bexleyheath, south of London, I'm affectionately known by people locally as 'Witchypoo'!

But I am happy to say that people's attitudes are changing. In the last five years especially, I've noticed that people are less likely to condemn my gift – and me – solely on the basis that they don't understand it. It is only by slogging away, slog, slog, slog, that I've built up a reputation and won the kind of track record for success that makes people think twice before branding me a con artist.

I hope I am doing my bit to open people's minds to a world beyond what they can just see or touch. It is difficult opening the minds of people in authority but now, slowly, many people who used to be very rigid in their beliefs are realising that, perhaps, there is more to all this than they thought.

But it is still an uphill task. The problem is that it's very easy to knock and mock psychics and it is not helped by the fact that, because anyone can set themselves up as a psychic, there are quite a few charlatans around.

On the other side of the coin are the critics who actually make their living out of ridiculing the paranormal and trying to prove that all psychic phenomena is a load of codswallop.

King of this Heap has to be James Randi, the TV magician and self-styled debunker of anything paranormal.

I first met him when we both appeared on Derek Jameson's programme on Sky satellite TV. At the end of the show Derek sprang a surprise test on me. This is always happening to me; it happens almost every time I appear on a TV show. They never warn you they're going to do it but what they basically say is, 'OK, you've claimed to be psychic, to have special gifts, so if you're so clever then prove it to us.'

It is really very unfair because if you're in a TV studio and you have just done a show you haven't prepared your mind for psychic work. But to most TV people, psychics are fair game and, from their point of view, whether you pass or fail the test, it makes for good television.

In this case Derek threw me a bunch of keys and said, 'Nella, we're going to ask you to give us a demonstration right here and now. What can you tell us about the person who owns these keys?'

Immediately I took the keys I felt that there had been illness around this person, a serious illness, and I said so. Then I said, 'What the hell happened to your car, lad? I can see your car being taken into the garage. That was either yesterday or today.'

'Whose keys are these?' asked Derek and he called over the lead guitarist from the studio band.

'Has there been any illness around you recently?' Derek asked him.

'No,' he said. 'I'm quite fit.'

'How about your car?'

'Yes, you're right there,' he said. 'It was taken into the garage today because the clutch has gone.'

Derek smiled and turned to James Randi. 'Well, what do you think of that, James?'

Randi, predictably, looked unimpressed but said, 'Mmm, very impressive. I'd like to get Nella into a laboratory and test her properly.'

'No bloomin' chance, mate!' thought I.

I know a lot of people think that psychics like me should agree to some kind of laboratory test to somehow prove themselves. But I don't agree. I'm not a guinea pig or a rabbit and I don't want to be taken into a laboratory and studied as if I were an animal.

Why should I? Why should I go into a laboratory to prove something that I prove every day of my life, to people I don't give tuppence for? I respect my gift and I only use it for a really good reason, not to satisfy cranky people who want to waste time proving that something that does exist doesn't.

As soon as the programme went off air Randi disappeared. When he had gone this young man, the guitarist, came running up to me and put his hands up.

'Nella,' he said. 'I'm sorry, you were right. I have been ill. I've just got over pleurisy and really had it quite badly. Just then I forgot about it. If it had flashed into my mind I would have said something but it didn't.'

I told him not to worry. I knew I was right, he knew I was right and Derek Jameson, who was listening to the conversation, now knew I was right. That was enough.

Not long afterwards I was invited by Granada Television to appear on Randi's own show. Quite a few of us had been invited. There was myself and one or two other psychics. I knew Randi would do his best to make us all look like idiots but I wasn't going to turn down his invitation. I didn't want to give him the satisfaction of thinking I was afraid to appear.

So I duly travelled up to the studios in Manchester. The first time we met him was on set, on air.

When it came to my turn he led me to a glass table where they had laid out a number of objects all wrapped in polythene bags. One of these objects, he told me, had been used as a murder weapon and I had one minute to say which one.

I picked out two – one was a hammer, the other an axe. I put the hammer down. 'I don't see a crime with the hammer but I see it breaking glass.'

He said, 'The hammer hasn't been used to break glass.'

'Not yet, James,' I said. 'Not yet.'

But I held on to the axe, I wouldn't let the axe go.

Predictably enough, Randi made a big thing about the hammer that I had first picked up. He said it was brand new, it had just been bought from a shop and hadn't been used for anything whatsoever, let alone a murder.

He said nothing about the axe I was holding on to. But as the programme was transmitted, on the bottom of the screen it said the axe had been used in a murder. But the writing was so small you would have needed glasses to see it.

That was my two minutes gone. Everyone suffered in the same way. One girl was a psychic artist and she worked with a man who was a clairvoyant. She drew a face which she said she believed was the face of someone who had died, related to a member of the audience.

Randi said, 'Right now, all those of you in the audience who can look at this face and think it resembles someone you know who's now dead put up your hands.'

Dozens of them did, so that girl was humiliated too.

The same kind of thing happened to all the other guests on the show and this, thought Randi, proved that people who claimed to have psychic gifts were all cons. As if half an hour was enough to dismiss the entire subject of the paranormal! It seemed to me to be a complete farce.

But not all television programmes are as one-sided as Randi's and not all professional magicians are as dismissive of people like me.

Earlier this year I met a lovely man called David Berglas, head of the Magic Circle, when we appeared on a TV show called *Robson's People*.

The programme was made by Tyne Tees Television and hosted by Alan Robson and there were to be three guests; David Berglas, the magician – an amazing memory man who could remember whole chunks of *Yellow Pages* at a time – and me.

I travelled up to Newcastle, where the show was being filmed, with a feeling of dread. 'What are they going to throw at me this time?' I thought. But everyone was charming, including the magician. He did not say if he believed in psychic phenomena or not. He just put his point of view about what he did and allowed me to put mine and explain what I do. No one expected me to perform some kind of sudden psychic magic of my own and, hopefully, people who were watching at home actually learned something.

Doing psychic work on television is incredibly difficult. The atmosphere is not right, it is hard to concentrate and, of course, you are only ever given a very limited time to do anything. That said, I am the first to admit that sometimes I get it wrong.

For four months last year I had a regular weekly spot on TV AM, the breakfast TV station. I would arrive and, five minutes before we went on air, they would put an object such as a key or pen or watch in my hand and then I would have to go on and describe the owner. I wasn't told the sex of the person or anything about them whatsoever and, to be frank, I surprised myself how often I got it right.

But sometimes I got it quite spectacularly wrong. Once they gave me a pen and I said, 'Oh, this man is funny. This man could make me laugh. I think he's very, very tall and very, very funny.'

I was right. The man was a professional comedian . . . He was also a midget!

It is not funny when I am asked to do work for a newspaper and, when I see the end result in print, I discover they have either mis-quoted me or, worse, they have actually made some of it up.

That happened to me earlier this year and I was furious. I had been asked by *The Sun* newspaper to try and contact the spirit of news-paper tycoon Robert Maxwell who died in mysterious circumstances last November.

Multi-millionaire Maxwell, who owned the Mirror Group of newspapers and many other companies, died after going overboard from his luxury yacht *Lady Ghislaine* while he was cruising around the Canary Islands. The papers were full of the story at the time. Did he fall or was he pushed? Everyone wanted to know. And, when it was discovered he'd siphoned off hundreds of millions of pounds from his own companies' pension funds, everyone asked what had he done with the money?

I told *The Sun* I would do my best to contact him although, as I tell everyone, if a spirit doesn't want to come through, they won't, and there's nothing I can do about it.

In fact, once I started to concentrate on Maxwell, he came through quite quickly and very clearly. I had the feeling he didn't want to talk to me but, in some way, he had no choice. For some reason he had to come back.

He looked much fatter than his pictures suggested. He looked big in all the photos in the newspapers but, close to, he was really bloated. I knew immediately I did not like this man. I didn't like the feel of him. The only good thing I can think to say about him is that he smelt nice, as if he was wearing a very expensive aftershave. That smell was strong and quite distinctive.

As he talked to me I felt afraid. This was not a good man at all. He said he did not fall overboard and he did not jump. When I asked him if he had committed suicide he became quite abusive and called me a 'stupid woman', something he kept bellowing at me at the end of almost every sentence.

'I am not a coward,' he said. 'Try again.'

When I asked if he had been murdered his face contorted into a horrible grin and his image disappeared for two hours. When he came back he refused to say any more about how he died saying only, 'There is great danger.' I didn't know what he meant, but in a way I could understand, because I felt danger too.

He was furious when I suggested he had stolen the pension fund money.

'I did not steal anything. I just used it,' he said.

'If I had been able to complete what I set out to do nobody

would have lost out, but the big boys lost their nerve.'

When I asked him the multi-million dollar question, 'Where is the money?' his image disappeared again and I couldn't get him back until the next day.

I kept asking him where the missing millions were until he finally said, 'There are millions of pounds held in the money warehouse in America.'

'What did he mean by the money warehouse?'

'You stupid woman, *money* warehouse,' he said with the emphasis on the word money.

'Where in America is this warehouse?' I asked.

For a while he was silent then he said, 'It's better for you that you don't find out.'

The way he talked frightened me. He was on odious man. Throughout our talk he used foul language, most of which I couldn't repeat here, and he was pompous and arrogant. He respects his wife very much, and he adores his daughter Ghislaine, but he is not in the slightest bit concerned about the suffering he has brought on his own family, or any one else for that matter.

Many people's natural instinct, when they have passed over to the other side and they can look back and see what devastating results their actions have had, is to come back and try and help the people they've hurt. But not Maxwell – no way. Spiriturally, he has a very long road to travel.

When I said to him, 'How do you feel about being called the biggest crook in the world?' he wasn't the slightest bit bothered.

Instead, he said to me, 'Well, one thing, they'll never forget they knew Robert Maxwell.'

I was glad when the contact with Maxwell ended and I would certainly never want to contact him again. It was not a pleasant experience.

The newspaper printed most of what I told them accurately enough but I was furious when I saw a paragraph at the end of the story. What did Maxwell think of the *Daily Mirror*, the paper once owned by Maxwell and the arch-rival publication of *The Sun*?

He is supposed to have replied, 'One of my big disappointments is that I never managed to make it a great paper like *The Sun*.' Codswallop! He never said any such thing to me and I never asked him any such question. No doubt *The Sun* thought that little bit of fiction was a huge joke but it made me look a fool. It also made it look as if the rest of the interview was equally ludicrous. In fact I am sure I must have touched a raw nerve somewhere with something I said, although I'm not sure what, and I don't want to know.

The day after the story about Maxwell appeared in the paper I received a phone call from a woman. She asked if I was Nella Jones and I said I was. She refused to give her name and she then said that she was a friend of Robert Maxwell and that I was to steer clear of him and not to try and find out any more about what had happened to the stolen money. Otherwise, she made it clear, I would be killed.

A day later I received a similar call, this time from a man. I was terrified. I was in absolutely no doubt that they meant business and the police took the threats very seriously indeed. Apart from keeping a close watch on the house for a long time, all my phone calls were intercepted.

So, while many other people were joking about my contact with Maxwell, some people somewhere were taking it very seriously indeed. But they need not worry. I have no intention of getting in touch with that awful man again.

One programme I did enjoy was Robert Kilroy-Silk's morning show on BBC earlier this year. There is a long way to go before any programme will have the courage to say to their audience, 'Look, we believe this woman. This is what she can do,' but at least the Kilroy show was well balanced.

As I said on the show, I am convinced that very soon there will be scientific proof that psychic power does exist. I'm keeping my eye on scientists at Cambridge University who work in quantum physics. I don't pretend to understand what they do, or how they work, but I think they are coming very close to the breakthrough.

Give them a year, maybe two, and they will have the proof. And when that happens it is going to make people rethink the whole world. The way we look at our lives will have to change and it will change. Sceptics will not doubt scorn this idea but I say, 'Remember, it wasn't so very long ago that people thought the world was flat.' And I am sure that the rethink will be on a similar scale to the one when people had to come to terms with the fact that the world is round.

Most sceptics are non-believers on the ridiculous basis that if you can't see something, or you can't actually hold it in your hands and touch it, then it can't exist. This of course is utter nonsense. Look back at your own life: what you remember most vividly and value most are probably those things that you couldn't see or touch.

No doubt you remember times of sorrow and sadness and times when you've been in pain; not the pain of a broken leg but the pain of rejection or loss. And, equally, you look back and smile at times of laughter and joy. At the end of life, when we look back, we all agree that what mattered most, what brought us the greatest happiness, was love. Loving and being loved.

You can't see love. You can't touch love. But who could honestly say that love doesn't exist?

Imagine that feeling of love, feel it coming out of you and going to the person you love. Even if you cannot touch that person, even if they are thousands of miles away, the love you are sending to them is a real living thing. You cannot see that love-link but nothing can break it – not even death.

Psychics like myself who can contact the dead are sometimes

accused of somehow taking advantage of the bereaved or making them feel even worse by saying their loved one's spirit is around them. The suggestion is that if the bereaved person thinks the loved one is still around, they won't grieve properly or come to terms with the death.

Obviously, I don't agree with that at all. In fact, I believe I help people to grieve and to face the loss of their loved one. Grief, like happiness, is only a state of mind. The bereaved person has to ask themselves, 'What am I grieving for?' The answer is that they are grieving the physical loss of a person.

They think, 'I'm not going to see him again, I will never be able to touch or hold him again.'

When they accept that, they grieve. But if they also come to understand that, even in death you can't break the love-link between you, it is an enormous comfort.

When I give someone proof by saying little things that only he or she and the loved one could have known, they know the link hasn't been broken. Of course, that helps them. I have had people cry with happiness when they have suddenly had proved to them that the link is still strong, still alive if you like. Then they know that the person has not simply vanished off the face of the earth, in spirit, in love, they are still here.

One case particularly sticks in my mind, probably because the couple were so young. He was a good-looking young man who, like so many others, just turned up for a sitting. I didn't know his name. I didn't know anything about him. But almost as soon as he sat down I saw an attractive young woman standing beside him, smiling, and she immediately started speaking to me.

'Tell him to take the heather plant from the draining board and put it where he wanted to put it in the first place,' she said. As usual, the message meant nothing to me but the young man burst into tears.

He looked at me and said, 'Who's telling you all this?'

I said, 'She says her name is Heather.'

'That's my wife,' he cried. 'I've just lost her.'

'Well,' I said. 'Don't waste time. She says you bought a pot of heather and now it's just sitting on the draining board.'

Then Heather started talking to me again.

'By the way, my little rose bush is covered up.'

'We haven't got a rose bush,' he said.

'Yes, we have,' Heather told me. 'It's outside the kitchen window. There's a big shrub that's overgrown there and if he looks under it he'll find the miniature rose I planted.'

Then she started to talk about their children and all the things they'd been up to. It was as if they were having a conversation and I was merely the interpreter. Finally, Heather turned her attention to me. She was worried.

'He's lonely now and I don't want him to be lonely. I want him to be happy,' and she went on to say that he would meet someone else, a lady with the initial 'J', and that they would be extremely happy together.

'And tell him I won't mind. I'll be happy that he's happy,' said Heather.

The young man was in tears again. 'But I'm still in love with Heather,' he said adamantly, 'I couldn't marry anyone else.'

'Well, let's wait and see,' I said.

At the end of the sitting he couldn't stop thanking me.

'My God, how you've lifted me,' he said. 'You've really lifted me.'

He went home and later he telephoned me. He had looked under the shrub outside the kitchen window and found the miniature rose that Heather had planted. We kept in touch and a couple of years later he phoned me to say that he and a girl called Judy were getting married.

'And I know Heather will be happy for me,' he said. 'You'll never know what you've done for me Nella, how you helped me.'

Some people come back again and again to contact their loved ones. I have one lovely elderly gent called Reg who comes to see me every month or so and those sittings are extraordinary.

He comes to contact his wife, Eileen. The first time he visited, Eileen came through to me straight away. 'Tell him he'd better say goodbye to Fred,' she said.

'What does she mean,' said Reg. 'The only Fred I know is fine so where's he going?'

A week later Fred was dead.

Another time Eileen said to me, 'Peggy's going over shortly.'

I said, 'That's the message Reg. Peggy's going over there shortly.'

Reg said he didn't know a Peggy but ten days later he telephoned me. 'You remember Eileen said Peggy was going over shortly. Well my daughter-in-law's mother Margaret has just died. It turns out she was known as Peggy.'

Reg and Eileen have very cosy domestic conversations through me. He doesn't speak much but Eileen does and she advises him. Back in the late summer, she was disgusted because their windows hadn't been cleaned and the curtains hadn't been washed.

'Oh heavens,' said Reg, 'She always was very fussy about her windows.'

She says lots of different things, usually about what Reg has been doing during the week, things incidentally I could not possibly know. She will say, 'Reg, I saw that and you did this and you shouldn't have done that.'

For Reg, his meetings with Eileen are a great comfort. He knows that she is there with him and he is not so lonely any more. When he first came to see me he was on the point of suicide, he said he just couldn't live without her. And Reg is typical of many of the people who come to see me. The sittings didn't delay his grief, or stop him grieving for the fact that physically Eileen was no longer with him, but before he made contact with her he didn't want to go on living. Like so many other bereaved people, he looked ahead and all he could see before him was a vast nothing, a road to nowhere.

Now he is fine. When you give people proof of this other existence they feel great. Of course, it does not stop them missing the person they have loved and lost. Of course not. But at least they know that there is a life after death and they are eventually going to see their loved one again, but on another plane. And *knowing* it means that until that time comes, they can get on with their own life – that's the important thing.

Many times I have had people come to see me who have lost a child and those sittings are always terribly emotional. Losing a child is the worst loss of all. During the Kilroy programme, a psychologist said people like me did positive harm in these cases because often the bereaved parents told their other children that the brother or sister they had lost had not really gone away but was there, in spirit, with them.

This frightened the other children so much that they couldn't come to terms with the death of their brother or sister, with the result that they became psychologically disturbed.

I have never known of a case like that personally, but I can say that I never give a reading to anyone under eighteen years old and I am sure other responsible psychics and spiritualists would say the same. If the bereaved parents think that their other children can handle the idea of life after death and the spirit world, then that's up to them. It is purely the parents' decision. A medium or clairvoyant wouldn't tell a child anything. It is up to the parents who, after all, know their children better than anyone else. That said, I have known several cases where the parents haven't said anything to the other children but the brother or sister has appeared in spirit to them, so *they've* told the parents.

Many of our critics say that it is simply not healthy for people to visit psychics, that people can become dependent on the psychic and this stops them from leading their own life and making their own decisions.

This is a tricky problem. I have had clients who start to become obsessive about the readings. They reach a stage where they admit they won't make a move without my say-so. This doesn't happen often because, usually, I can see the warning signs and put a stop to it.

Often someone will come again and again because they are trying to make me say what they want to hear. Perhaps a man they have loved has left them and they want me to say that he is going to come back. They are living in hope and they think, if they come often enough, eventually I'll be able to tell them that he will return.

When I think this might be happening, I say to them, 'Wait, slow down for just a minute. This may be what you think you want right now, but if you give yourself time you might realise that's not what you really want, or that is not what's best for you.'

Or, as often happens, they will come to me and say, 'I was so happy with this man but he's left me. Now I don't believe in God because I prayed that this man would come back and he hasn't.'

I say, 'That's got nothing to do with it. It's not God's fault.'

However frequently they visit me, I don't tell them what they want to hear. I can't do that. I tell them what comes through to me and what I can see and it doesn't always please them. Part of my job is to help people help themselves. I am not going to lead their life for them.

First of all I try to give them an insight into themselves; to get to know themselves and, once they've taken a good look at themselves, I ask them, 'What are you hoping for is for this or that to happen, for this person or that person. But are you sure it's not because you're feeling so weak and vulnerable that you want to cling to this person?'

I try to help them to become more independent, to stand on their own two feet, to do different things. I say, 'Do such and such and you'll gain the respect of everybody, not just the man you're after.'

Of course, when someone is in a vulnerable state – and many are when they come to see a psychic – it would be very easy to deceive them. But I don't believe in conning people, even if it's done with the very best motives. It would be very easy to tell people only what they want to hear, especially if they are upset and you know that telling them what they want to hear would cheer them up and put a smile back on their face.

But I never do it. In the long run it's not a good idea. Honesty, however painful, really is the best and only policy.

By deceiving someone you are not helping them and that, after all, is what I'm here for. My clients know, that when they come to me, they get the truth – and they are not stupid. Non-believers never stop making out that people who visit psychics are, at best, misguided and, at worst, gullible fools. That's rubbish.

Most are ordinary rational souls who need guidance in some area of their life. I have just as many men coming to see me as women. It's certainly not a case of my merely seeing dozens of women who are neurotic because they've lost a man!

Some come because they are about to make a business move or change their job. They come because they're worried about their children or their bank balance, they come with all kinds of problems. They want guidance and we psychics don't just act as therapists, we have that little bit of extra insight to show them. We can say, 'Well, if you do this, that's going to happen or if you do that, this is going to happen. Take your pick. You've got the choice.' Everyone still has free will.

Many people want to believe in life after death and they want to believe that people like me can see into the future. The sceptics will say that, because they want to believe so much, after their reading their memory conveniently plays tricks on them and they convince them-selves I've been accurate when I haven't. In other words, they exagger-ate what I have said in their own minds and they bend the message from the sitting and all that I have told them so that it fits the truth.

But my clients don't have to rely on memory alone to recall what I have told them because I always tape every sitting. Any psychic worth his or her salt tapes every reading and, if you are planning to visit a psychic, I strongly advise you to take a tape and tape recorder with you if they are not already provided.

So often, someone will see a psychic and it will all stay clear in their mind for a day or two and then they forget. It is always a good idea to replay your tape when you get home because there will be things said that didn't sink in at the time. It's a bit like going to the doctor. It is always hard to concentrate and fully take in what he's say-ing, especially if you're feeling down and anxious. Anyway, it is inter-esting to play the tape back a month or two later to see what has come true and what has yet to happen

If you do forget, there would be no point in asking *me* for a verbal replay. I rarely remember what I've said. After the sitting I push it all out of my mind. I couldn't keep it all in my head, or I'd go mad.

One of the biggest 'cons', according to the critics, are psychic meetings in halls. I used to hold meetings like that for healing but had to give it up because I couldn't afford to keep going. As I don't charge for healing I had to find the money to hire the hall myself and it all got too much. But I have done several psychic sessions in halls with about three or four hundred people in the audience.

I encountered one man on a TV programme who said that the way we psychics worked the so-called 'scam' at these meetings was to look through the obituary columns of the local newspapers before we started and remember a few names of the recently deceased. Then, once we are up there on the podium, we can say, 'Does anyone here know Fred Bloggs?' And since someone there is bound to know Fred Bloggs, a local man who died, it makes us look very good indeed!

Well I cannot speak for other mediums or psychics, but I have never done that and I do not know of any good psychic who has. When I am up there I look around the crowd and sometimes a voice tells me to look towards one certain person in the audience or, for some reason, I feel drawn to that person. Then, I always keep to specifics as they are given to me. It might start with something small like, 'You were out yesterday and you bought a new duvet.'

Then, if the spirit tells me I am talking to the right person, I can go onto more meaningful matters. But you can't tell me that half the audience had been out the previous afternoon shopping for a duvet. That would be ridiculous!

The other criticism is that the psychic or medium will plant people in the audience, people they've already met and talked to, so that they can look good when they appear to know so much about someone.

I have never done that, nor ever would, but I can see how it sometimes happens unintentionally. I see so many people I could not possibly remember all of their faces and, once I've seen them, I usually forget almost immediately what I have told them.

If they have been pleased with the reading I have given them, and then they hear I'm holding a session in the local hall, it's hardly surprising that they come along. Maybe I will recognise them, more likely I won't, and I have no real control over who I am drawn to when I start the meeting. That is not up to me, it is up to the spirits who come through. So you can see how it could happen.

It always makes me sad that some of the most virulent critics of psychics like myself are men of the church. Catholic priests, in particular, seem to find our work odious and say it is the work of the devil. Then there are the evangelists, the bible thumpers. Some of them say we speak with forked tongues and some, I am sure, would delight in bringing back the stake and the old witches' ducking stools, the ones they used to hang over rivers back in the Dark Ages. The so-called witch was tied into the stool and ducked in the water. If she held her breath for long enough and survived she was obviously a witch, so she was then burnt at the stake. If she drowned it proved she wasn't a witch – but of course she was dead anyway!

These people's minds are so blocked off, and their view of the future is so blinkered, sometimes I despair. I can say, in all honesty, I haven't a clue why some people in the church find people like me such a threat because there are many who are sympathetic to what we do.

You don't have to be religious to be psychic, and vice versa. I've known atheists who are psychic. Your psychic power, I believe, has nothing to do with which religion you follow, if any.

Personally I am very religious. I am a Christian and I have a deep faith in a Christian God. I think I became religious when I was very young because I realised that the power I had was so awesome. It was so big, so miraculous. I thought to myself, 'This power; it must come from somewhere. I don't know what it is. I don't know why it's been given to me. But it's so powerful it must come from God.'

My psychic ability simply enhanced my belief in God. But I believe that we are all psychic whether we believe in God or not – whether you are a Christian, Jew, Muslim, Buddhist, Hindu, atheist or agnostic.

We all use our psychic abilities to a certain extent. Even atheists pray; they can't help themselves. We all pray and, whether you are in church on Sunday or you are praying at home alone, you are using your psychic power, even if intellectually you deny its existence.

All religions believe in the power of prayer but what are you doing when you pray? Supposing there is someone you want to pray for. With the whole of your being, with your mind, with your heart, with your love, you want something to happen, for that person to be better or for things to be right in their life.

You call it prayer, but what you are actually doing is conjuring up this mystic power within yourself, your psychic self – that power you can use for good or for evil. I don't use it for evil because I love people, I love our world and I hope one day it will get back to being a beautiful world. I love to see people happy and it certainly wouldn't make me happy to see people unhappy.

I am afraid that a lot of people, with the same strength of psychic power as I have, do use it for evil. But I do believe that when someone gives out hate to another person they are really just destroying themselves. They may not realise it at the time, but that's what they're doing. Those who acknowledge the power but use it for evil will regret it in the end, because it will come back on them – maybe not in this life but certainly in the next.

I have never doubted my own psychic power. I have always accepted it. Sometimes that means I have felt lonely because no one else seems to understand what it's like.

But I have always accepted it: I haven't really had much choice. You should accept it too. Once you think about it, once you open your mind to it, many things in your life will become clearer.

For years, when I've talked to people about the psychic power within each and every one of us, I've felt as if I was banging my head against a brick wall. But minds are slowly but surely opening, thank God.

Of course, if you acknowledge your psychic strength, if you look at the world through your psychic eye, you can expect to be ridiculed. But often it is fear that makes people react that way. They don't understand it, so they fear it. We all have a basic fear of the unknown: it's only human.

It is difficult, as a psychic, to defend the entire psychic profession. How can I defend and justify the work of all the psychics, mediums, clairvoyants and healers in the country or the world? Impossible. And the sad truth is that just one or two charlatans give us all a bad name.

I believe that a responsible, honest clairvoyant or psychic, can do a lot of good in the world and help a great many people in a great many ways. The problem, as you are probably already thinking, is how do you know that the psychic you are planning to visit is good and honest?

It's very difficult to judge. Some who advertise are good: some who advertise are not so good. How are you to know? And if you are planning to visit a psychic because of a personal problem that is distressing you and you are feeling vulnerable, someone who doesn't know what they are talking about might distress you further.

Personally, I never advertise. Everyone who comes to me comes through word of mouth. They hear about me one way or another – often I'm not sure how they have heard. If you haven't been to a psychic before I think personal recommendation is really the best way to do it. Ask around.

If someone has been to a psychic and what the psychic has said has come true, they will tell people. If you don't know anyone who has been to a psychic, don't pluck a name out of a magazine. Without feedback you could be wasting your money: wait until you do hear of a good one.

The trouble is that the psychic business can so easily be exploited by con-merchants. At the moment, anyone can set themselves up as a clairvoyant or healer or psychic with impunity. It's all wrong.

What I, and many other psychics, would really like to see is a register, maybe compiled by one of the leading psychic organisations in the country, of authentic psychics, those who have been tested and proved. At least then people would have somewhere to go, a list to check which maybe wouldn't be a guarantee of excellence or accuracy but, at least, they would know they were not going to a con merchant.

It hasn't happened yet but I am confident it will. One day.

Of course everyone will still be at liberty to go and see the psychic housewife around the corner – after all that's how I started! But it would be some kind of safeguard against vulnerable people being exploited.

NINE

You and Your Psychic Gift

'Psychic: sensitive to phenomena lying outside range of normal experience; of soul or mind; that appears to be outside the region of physical law.'

COLLINS ENGLISH DICTIONARY

I am psychic. You are psychic. So, too, are your children, your family, your friends . . .

I believe, with an absolute certainty, that there is psychic ability in each and every one of us. The only difference between you and I is that I use my psychic power – it is so strong I have no choice but to use it, but you probably don't, at least not as much as you could.

The wonderful thing about being psychic is that it is not something you have to swot up on. The power is already all there inside but after years of being smothered by the worries and trappings of everyday life it has become buried deep within you. What you have to do is to dig down deep within yourself and bring your psychic self back to the surface.

There are no rigid rules – we are all different. And there are no hard and fast lessons to learn, or lines to write. Using you psychic gift is about looking at life in a different way and, if you can discover your psychic self and become more aware of your spiritual side, you will lead a much fuller and more rewarding life.

I don't believe one type of person is more likely to be psychic than another. There is no one typical personality who is psychic because we all are.

But you frequently find that the top psychics, those who are highly respected and make a living out of their gift, have lived a hard life and have suffered in some way. Often, their personal lives haven't been happy. I am not quite sure why this is, but it seems to be the case with most of the really good psychics I have known. Perhaps what makes them so good is that, because they've suffered in life themselves, they can more easily understand suffering in others.

But that does not mean that if you have led a reasonably tranquil and happy life you cannot be psychic or make the most of your psychic abilities. Of course you can!

I also think that often it is the simpler people who find it easier to dig up their psychic selves. By that I do not mean unintelligent people, merely people who look at life in a simple way, accepting there is right and wrong, good and bad. People who live very complex lives, and see all life through a permanent web of complication, have a more difficult road to travel because, in trying to make the most of your psychic self, you are trying to recapture your early innocence, your wonder at the world, that childlike ability to open your mind.

When we are children we know much more than we think we do; as adults we know so much less than we think we do!

When we are children we are often astounded by what we see. We don't understand most of it but we know the world is a magical place – that is what we are trying to get back to.

Remember, when you were a child, how excited you were when it snowed? Remember the joys of jumping in puddles and how astonished you were when you first saw the sea?

Now, when it snows, you probably worry about the pipes in the attic bursting; you don't jump in puddles because you don't want to get your shoes wet and, when you're at the seaside, you are mainly worried about how cold the water is and whether you have remembered to bring you sunglasses.

Think about it for a while.

Whatever nationality you are, whichever race you belong to, nothing makes any difference to your psychic power – age, looks, wealth are all irrelevant.

No one nation or people are more psychic than any other. There's a common idea that the people from the East are more psychic than we are but I don't believe that is true at all. They appear to be more psychic only because, to make a huge generalisation, they place more emphasis on the spiritual side of life and look at life in a different, maybe a more sensible, way to us here in the West.

And I do not believe that religion comes into being psychic. It does not matter what religion you are. Your faith in God and your psychic ability are two completely different things. Personally, I claim to be a Christian. I try to live a Christian life, doing what I believe is right, but that has nothing to do with my psychic power, absolutely nothing. It wouldn't matter if I was an aetheist, I would still be as psychic as I am now.

So what we are talking about here is not you and your relationship with God, however you perceive Him – or Her – to be. This is something else completely.

Diehard scientists say we only have five senses; we can see, hear, smell, touch and taste. Those who believe in psychic power say that people who are psychic have a sixth sense. I believe we have *all* got that sixth sense. I would go further, I think that we have probably got a seventh, eighth, ninth . . . and maybe more which have yet to come to light.

Even if you don't accept the idea that you have got a sixth sense, you are probably using it every day unknowingly.

It's the little things: you think about someone you haven't heard from for ages and the next minute or the next morning the phone rings and it's them. Unconsciously, you have been using your sixth sense to send a message to them to get in touch. In fact, you can use this quite easily and consciously.

If you really want to contact someone – I mean really contact them because it's important to speak to them and not just for frivolous reasons – picture the person in your mind, picture them standing before you but a long way off. Slowly bring the image of the person closer and closer until they are standing in front of you. Then tell them that you would like them to get in touch. They will.

Using your sixth sense, that extra sense, means more than just accepting its existence. It means looking at life in a different way – quite literally. Most people look at life from a few feet above ground level. It is not just that they are only concerned with the things in life that effect them directly, to the exclusion of all else; they only look at life from the ground. How many people ever look up? How many times do you raise your eyes from the ground and look up or around at the world about you?

Most people look at the world from a permanent height of five feet five inches or however tall they are. They're far too busy rushing down the street to this shop or that office and, what they do see, doesn't register because their mind is full of what they have to do: what the boss thinks of them, what they're going to cook for dinner tonight, what their lover or children are up to, what's going to happen next . . . They are so busy thinking about trivialities that they don't take time to look up, around or inside.

And that is one of the secrets of making the most of your psychic self. You must learn to look, but more than that you must learn to *see*.

Just as people don't look properly at the world around them neither do they take the time to look inside themselves. They ignore their feelings, they are too busy, they shove their feelings to one side. But you shouldn't ignore any emotion that you feel.

When I say look inside yourself I don't mean you should go around for twenty four hours a day analysing what you feel about every little thing that happens to you, because if you do you will end up screwed up like a corkscrew and go completely potty!

What I am talking about is being 'in touch' with your feelings. So many people have lost touch with themselves. Suddenly, after years, maybe at a time of crisis, they *do* look inside themselves and they're shocked. They hardly recognise themselves and what kind of person they've become and they think, 'Heavens, how did I get like this?'

But you can prevent that happening. For example, say you are having a cup of tea, doing nothing in particular, and suddenly a little grain of sadness crosses your mind. Most people ignore that grain. You can see them sometimes even physically shake their head to get rid of it. But don't ignore it. Think of that grain. Think, 'Why did that feeling of sadness come to me? What was it connected with?' Don't ignore it, investigate it so you bring it out rather than try to smother it inside.

Looking inside yourself does not mean dwelling on your faults, thinking what a terrible person you are, or how you've behaved like an idiot. We all do silly things at times and we all make mistakes. Looking inside yourself is not about making yourself more depressed or worried than you might be already – in fact it means the opposite. It means 'lifting your spirit', and if you find that difficult to do from scratch there are a couple of practical things you can do with your mind that will make you feel better.

Imagine that, some distance in front of your eyes, there are two empty frames hanging suspended in the air. One is black and one is white. Concentrate on the white frame. Look at that white frame, pour all your love and direct all your actions into that frame and consciously push the black frame out of the way. The white frame is a lovely frame, it's safe, and acts as a protection from the black frame. Push the black frame away until it's no longer in your sight, then centre the white frame in your line of vision.

We all get low at times. Someone said that most men lead lives of quiet desperation and, unfortunately, I think that it is true. These days we are always being told how important it is to relax, but most people if they are honest admit that firstly, they haven't got the time and secondly, they haven't really the first idea how to go about it.

But I believe that by using your psychic power you can feel better, the whole perspective of life changes and you can lift yourself out of depression. With practice you can, for a while, push the blackness away and replace it with something else; if not pure happiness then something that's maybe even more valuable – peace.

When you are depressed here is something to try. It doesn't take long; you don't have to do or wear anything special; in fact all you need is somewhere quiet to be alone for a while and, if you can't even take five minutes for it during the day, try it when you're in bed at night before you drift off to sleep.

Sit or lie down, close your eyes and imagine you are going on a journey. Other worries may intrude but push them away. You are going on a journey. It will not take long. You are coming with me, you are walking beside me. We are not rushing. We are walking quietly, evenly. We are going through a gate into a beautiful garden. It is hushed, it is evening and it is warm. It has been a hot sunny day and now the light is fading but the air is still warm.

You can smell the grass, freshly mown, and you're taking your shoes off and walking barefoot on the grass. It is warm and comfortable and the grass is soft. You can smell the sweet scent of the roses and the honeysuckle. You're walking across the spring grass towards a pretty white-painted bench, where you are going to sit down.

You sit down on the bench, it's soft and comfortable, and you sit there enjoying the cool breeze and the perfume of the flowers. You're grateful to be taking a little time off from your worries. It feels good to take this break. Your worries are left behind in the other world. You are having a rest and, from somewhere close by, you can hear the sound of water. It may be a fountain or a stream. You feel content. It's your secret garden.

Now, into the garden, very slowly, very gently, walks a figure, a friendly figure. The figure can be anyone you want it to be, a man or a woman, a stranger. The figure is walking up to you and smiling and you're happy to see this person. The figure gives you a gift. You accept the gift and the figure slowly leaves the garden.

The feelings you have are all contentment and the gift gives you great pleasure. You look at it and then you slowly walk back into the house, the beautiful house this garden belongs to, and you sit in a cool room looking at your present.

You feel rested and much better than when you started your

journey. You wait for a minute or two, then you know it's time to go to your other home. You open your eyes and you are home.

This may all sound completely silly to you but, believe me, it isn't. The process isn't hypnosis, although hypnotists use similar techniques, and it is similar to a form of meditation too.

If you concentrate on your journey and give yourself up to it, if you go with it and do not fight it, you will start to relax involuntarily and you will find it makes you feel better, it lifts your spirit. After this, whenever you are depressed, you can go off to your secret garden for a few minutes.

Being in the garden helps you to get rid of all the stress in your mind, because you are at peace. It is also interesting for you to think about who the figure was. Was it male or female? You mustn't sit there thinking 'Um . . . I'd like him or her to turn up in my secret garden . . .' It's the figure that first comes into your mind that matters. And what was the gift? Think about that. The gift is symbolic of what you're really looking for at the moment. What was it? That's your secret.

Of course, you can say, the garden is all in my mind. I was just imagining. Were you? We all fantasise and usually we dismiss our fantasies as wishful thinking; we tell ourselves we're being stupid.

But imagination is important – it is a big part of ourselves, our inner selves. Imagination is the beginning of positive thought, part of what we imagine is the inner wish, the inner dream. Some of it, of course, is unrealistic and unattainable – that's one of the joys of imagination – but a lot of what you imagine you can turn into positive fact. 'Rubbish,' you might say. But think about it!

If you look at your sitting room you'll sometimes think, 'I need a change. If I put that there and move this to there . . .' and in your imagination you see how the room will look if you rearrange it. Similarly, if you look hard, you can see what your life will look like if you rearrange it.

So you must use your eyes along with your imagination. There is nothing foolish about using your imagination. It stretches your mind and, God knows, most of our minds need stretching beyond the things we can actually see and touch.

There is another point I want to make about your sixth sense. To be able to use your sixth sense to the full, you have really got to learn to use the other five fully. They are all an equal part of you and there is no point in concentrating on the sixth sense if you are ignoring the other five. They are all connected. Each is linked to the other. Each is a road to understanding the other.

It takes all six senses to look at the world and appreciate what it has to offer us. Most of us look – but we don't see. When did you last look at a tree except to give a passing thought 'That's a tree.'

Next time you look at a tree why don't you take the time to see it for what it is. First look at the base of it, look at the trunk, look how it has grown and curved over the years. Look at its branches spreading out – that represents its growth. It has been growing there for years and years – probably all the time that you've been growing. It is almost on a human plane with us. It is growing, it is alive, it is breathing just like us, it is living. Whenever I see a beautiful tree I want to go and touch it and feel the life from that tree.

Once you really look at a tree in that way you'll probably feel the same urge. It may sound pseud or cranky, but the more you think about it the more you'll realise I'm right.

Just about everything out there is living; living and breathing, just as we are. We might fleetingly think, 'Oh that's a pretty red flower' or 'that's a very green tree.' But that is all we allow ourselves time to think. No one seems to have time any more to see, to feel, to really look, and yet these are very basic elements in life. We have become blind. We don't use our senses any more and as a result our senses have become dead, including our sixth sense and our psychic selves. If you want to use the psychic gift you've been given you've got to *wake up*!

Why are so many people, especially young people, turning to alcohol and drugs these days; things that induce an artificial sense of pleasure, oblivion or peace? It is because the normal senses they were given at birth are dead.

There's nothing spooky or cranky about this. It is merely common sense. And it makes me very angry that even people who pay lip service to so-called green issues are usually too busy rushing off to a Save the Planet rally to actually stop and look around them, look up or look inside.

When you feel bad in life the best thing you can do is to go back to the basic senses. You have the sense of touch. Be aware of that sense of touch. You pick up a cup and saucer – you're touching it but you probably don't take time to feel it. Is it rough or is it smooth? When you use your sense of touch you think, 'Yes, that feels nice.' Once you begin to consciously use your senses, you will be surprised what a difference it makes to your life.

Even at home, doing household chores, you can turn something that was just a drag before into something much more pleasurable. Many women feel trapped at home running the family and get terribly depressed and bored. If that is you, then try going back to the basics. When you are washing up don't just think, 'God, I hate doing this, I'm bored.' Think how your hands feel in the warm soapy water, it's a good, sensual feeling.

You touch the china in the sink and it feels good; you pick up a clean tea cloth and wipe it until it sparkles and it looks good. Take it all in, don't just do things automatically, like a robot.

Most people are becoming just like robots these days. But it doesn't need much extra time to let yourself enjoy what you're doing. Don't plod through life like an unfeeling robot. Humans are supposed to live a full life but only you can make your life fuller and richer. Live

a full life, grow, and you will have an empathy with every living, growing thing around you. What if life is difficult? Yes, it can be difficult.
But remember it is a privilege to be here and we should feel very humble that we have been given time to spend on what was, and still
mainly is, a beautiful planet. We have the senses of touch, and smell
and taste and feel and sight, which should not be dismissed as though
they were nothing. These are the greatest gifts that man can have and
until you can learn to appreciate the first five senses, how are you going
to go on to make the most of your sixth sense, and perhaps the seventh
and eighth?

To make the most of your psychic gift, first of all go back to
basics. Start at square one. Just putting on a clean pair of socks in the
morning can be a lovely experience. You can feel the soft sock going
over your foot and you feel the leather of your shoe. It feels good. Once
you have recaptured your senses you can move on to look at your sixth
sense in depth.

These days you can hardly move in the streets for people jogging
or cycling and, wherever we turn, we're being encouraged to exercise
and to feel positively guilty if we don't. Well, that is all well and good.
Of course, exercise helps us to keep our physical selves healthy. But
what about our spiritual selves? To keep our physical body working in
reasonably good order we need to use it. Anyone who has ever been ill,
lying in bed for a few weeks, and who has then tried to stand up knows
that your legs go all weak and wobbly from lack of exercise.

It is the same with our spiritual selves. The spiritual 'you' needs
exercising too. Exercising our spiritual selves is just as important as
exercising our physical selves. We spent very little time looking at ourselves, looking inside ourselves. Yet doing that isn't being self indul-
gent, it is healthy and, to make the most of your psychic gift, you have
got to do it.

I don't like to use the term 'spiritual exercises' which suggests a
kind of spiritual aerobics! I prefer to call them self-exercises, life exercises. Spend some time just sitting and looking, feeling, sensing. Get
your other five senses heightened and start to look around you. Make a
conscious effort to really see what you're looking at – just the simple
things. Perhaps you have a pot plant in your sitting room. You've
probably never looked at it, not really. Spend a couple of minutes looking at its form and shape and colour. Look at the light and shade.
Imagine you are a painter and you are going to reproduce this plant on
paper. Look at the veins on its leaves, study it.

In summer, walk barefoot whenever you can. I love walking barefoot in the summer just to feel the earth under my feet. You feel completely different barefoot and whenever I go to the country I'm always
compelled to pick up a handful of earth and smell it, especially after
rain when it smells wonderful. Of course, some people think I'm crazy,
but I don't give a damn about that and why should you?

What you're doing with all this exercise is making yourself more aware. Probably, like most people, you've got out of the habit of using your senses to the full and of looking around you. When you were a baby and a small child you did it all the time, quite naturally and instinctively, and that's what you're trying to get back to.

The pace and stresses of modern life conspire against you using your five senses to the full which means it's less easy to use your psychic power, your sixth sense. Even when people are not working frantically, like hamsters on a wheel, what do they do to relax? If they are not jogging madly they are sitting goggle-eyed in front of the television.

I believe that watching too much TV dulls all your senses, including your psychic sense, because you are not thinking or feeling for yourself. Everything you feel, or see, is coming at you second-hand. You watch the screen and you might sense strong emotions like anger, sympathy, love, hate. But they are all being portrayed by someone else. It's not you. You are feeding off someone else's emotions and feelings. They are not your feelings – the ones you are trying to get in touch with. Of course, I'm not saying that if you want to make the most of your psychic gift you can't watch telly! That would be ridiculous. I enjoy TV myself. All I am saying is that you shouldn't build your life around the front room and the television every evening. Start living for yourself and, especially if you're feeling down in the dumps, do something. Don't slump in front of the TV, do something. Go for a walk around the block, smell the night air, or clean your windows. You will feel you've achieved something and it will lift your spirit.

All this may sound simple advice. It is. But, if you put it into practice, very soon you will realise that your life has changed considerably. You will have changed too – not your basic personality, of course, but you are expanding you, expanding your life. And that is a key to your psychic self and making the most of your psychic gifts. You've got to open up your mind and open your heart.

After a while you are going to find you look at people in a different way. You will look at someone you have known for a long time and you will be more aware of them. You will notice more how they look because you have trained yourself to look more closely at every living thing. But, more than that, you will begin to sense things in others since your own senses have become heightened.

Your instincts about other people will become stronger. Whereas, before you might have said, 'Mary's in a grumpy mood today,' and then dismissed it, now you will instinctively look into her eyes and think, 'There's been an upset in Mary's life. There's sadness and confusion there.'

It may suddenly strike you that someone who always smiles, and has always appeared very happy and relaxed, is, in fact, suffering a deep unhappiness. Don't dismiss these instincts. Don't say, 'I'm imagining this.' You're not. What is happening is that, along with your other five senses, your sixth sense has also suddenly woken up.

You may look at someone and suddenly find yourself thinking

'Hospital' or 'Baby' or 'Pain in foot.' Don't immediately push those thoughts out of your mind. Don't, of course, pounce on the person concerned and say, 'What does hospital mean to you? Or baby? Or pain in left foot?' You could unintentionally upset someone very much.

Perhaps they've just visited a sick friend in hospital, maybe they've just lost a baby or can't have one, or maybe the pain in the left foot is something that is causing them great discomfort and they don't want to talk about it. You must tread very carefully. Of course you will want to know if you are right but you can usually find that out in the course of normal conversation.

If you have reached this stage, don't be surprised if you feel much more emotionally vulnerable than you used to. You are not looking at people as mere blobs now. What they give to you is not what is important. You have learned not just to look at them but to *see* them for what they are – a soul just like you. You can see the world through their eyes and feel what they are feeling more easily.

When something awful has happened to someone I try to feel it too. It all boils down to that four letter word again – love. If you love your fellow human beings, whenever they are suffering you take it on board, you feel it. It doesn't take the pain away from them but it does mean you are sharing it with them, you are sharing the experience. And that helps. Most of us don't listen properly. We pretend to listen but we don't really.

Gradually, if you follow what I have been saying, you will increasingly come to realise that it is not what you get back that matters, it is what you give out. You see, love is worthless unless you give it away.

You will start to smile more. As you're walking down the street, and going into the shops, you'll be so much more aware of the world around you. And, when you see people, don't avoid their eyes. Look at them, smile, and say 'Good morning' or 'Hello.'

You would be quite amazed at what that does for people, it lifts their lives. You only have to think yourself how much better you feel when you go into a shop and someone greets you with a smile rather than a scowl. We are not islands. The vibrations we all pick up instinctively from other people affect our lives enormously.

Be the one to smile first and, even if you don't get a smile in return, you will feel better for it because you have given out some kind of positive psychic signal.

As you instinctively use your sixth sense more and more you will become not only more aware of other people – you will become more aware of the truth about yourself, the true you. You will begin to know yourself. Don't put yourself down and don't say that you know your limitations because human beings have no limitations, human beings can stretch themselves as high and as far as they choose.

But do get to know your weaknesses and face them. Your strengths you can always turn into greater strengths but know where your weaknesses lie. Do that and the strengths will grow automatically.

Once you start using all your six senses to the full you will be amazed at how much more vivid life becomes. You will see psychic colour and, believe me, there's no colour on earth to match it. It is pure, it is beautiful.

You will probably see psychic colours just before you go to sleep. You may see a flash of a strip of colour, maybe a blob of colour, maybe a circle but, once you have seen these colours, you will never forget them. And you will see more colour in everyday life; these will seem more sharp and pure too, and you will see depth, shades, lights, tones and undertones everywhere.

Of course, because you've woken up your whole self, you must be prepared to feel emotionally drained sometimes. Scientists say we only use one tenth of our brain. If you have got to this stage I believe you are now beginning to use that other nine-tenths – probably in a miniscule way, but at least you are using some of it.

It's important to take time for yourself to relax. I find that sitting in front of a living fire is very relaxing. Fire is warm and there is life within fire. If you are lucky enough to have a coal or log fire, take time to sit looking at the flames, lose yourself for a while, just five minutes will do. Don't think about the worries of the day and don't worry if your mind seems to travel off erratically at different tangents. If you find it going off in a direction you don't like, bring it back to the flame.

I use candles quite a lot in my work. If I have a very heavy prayer session – one where I have many prayers to say for many people in trouble – and I need to use my psychic power to the full, I will light a candle, not because there is any great significance in the candle itself, but because, for me, the important thing is that little bit of living light. I can concentrate on that light and, through the tiny flickers, I can see the Greater Light. The candle is my channel to the Greater Light. You don't really need candles for meditation but, if I am going way out on the psychic plane, I like to keep that candle burning. It guides me. It guides me out and it guides me back as well. Focussing on that flame brings me safely home where I should be.

You may also find that your dreams become more vivid and somehow more meaningful. I do think dreams are very important. If you have a vivid recurring dream you should keep pen and paper beside your bed, write it down and go and see one of those people who specialise in analysing dreams.

I am not an expert at interpreting dreams. There are people far better qualified than me. I can only tell you what I instinctively, psychically, feel. But they can tell you, after years of study, what various symbols mean; symbols which have been passed down over hundreds of years and which we use all the time without even realising we do so.

Funnily enough, I don't often dream. I mean, I don't often have dreams that I remember well. Most nights I wake up feeling I haven't dreamt at all. When I do dream, they are very vivid, but those are rare.

Some dreams have stuck in my mind and I still don't fully understand what they mean. I think the dreams we have in childhood are very important. I'm not quite sure why but maybe they are a pointer for the life we have to follow later. Many people who resist their psychic power get most of their psychic messages through their dreams. I think the reason I don't remember many dreams is because I get my dreams when I'm fully awake! I live permanently in a kind of twilight world.

The memories of dreams that we had when we were children must, I'm sure, be important. We all have them. Maybe they show our hopes, our fears, or maybe they show something more.

I had the most vivid dream of my life when I was about nine or ten and it has stayed with me ever since. In the dream, I was walking across a ploughed field and in the middle of the field was a boxing ring all set up for a major boxing competition.

There was a kind of festival atmosphere about the place, although there was no fair, just the boxing ring. There were lots of people watching the fight and I felt myself walk towards the ring to see what was going on.

When I got there I realised that all the people who were fighting in the ring were prisoners. They were convicts of some kind and they had been put in the ring against their will to entertain the local landlords and bigwigs.

I walked past the ring. They were just about to begin another fight and my eyes were drawn to one of the new contestants. He was dressed in rags. Our eyes met and in those eyes I saw such a great sadness that I felt desperate pity for him. I think of it now and I still feel this overwhelming sense of sadness. I had the dream again and again and I don't know if he won his fight, or what it meant, but the dream stuck. The only effect it had on me immediately – and I remember this quite clearly – was that when I saw someone sad I didn't ignore it. I thought of the sad boxer. Maybe the dream symbolised the constant battle of life, I don't know.

So, I really do believe that dreams should not be ignored, especially when you have just started making the most of your psychic power. Most are difficult to remember I know, but you will find that, surprisingly, some dreams stay with you during the day and these are the ones that you should make a note of. If you don't want to go to a professional dream interpreter, then write down everything you can remember, however silly it looks. Put your dream story away for a while then, days later, look at what you have written. You may very well be able to make more sense of it than anyone else could, once you actually start to think about it and look at it after sometime has elapsed. And, remember, psychic clues are just that – clues. They are not always designed to give you the answer straight away but to make you think and find the answer for yourself.

If dreams when you are asleep are important then your day-dreams, once you are using your psychic gift properly, become even more so. Once you've dug down deep and found that psychic power that lies inside all of us, you may be quite surprised by some things you experience. Don't dismiss them. I know I keep saying that, but I can never forget how you, and all of us, have been conditioned to ignore and ridicule any vision we don't fully understand that comes to us suddenly like a leaf on the breeze. It is there and then it is gone. Do not pretend you have not seen it at all. You have, you really have!

One strange thing that might happen to you is that you may get the feeling that you are 'not quite there'. I don't mean you're not quite right in the head! But you may feel that your body and the essential 'you', have briefly become separated. If you are using your psychic ability fully, there is nothing weird about it at all. It happens often but, understandably, it can be a bit alarming at first.

Once you have developed your psychic power to the full you can travel on the astral plane wherever you want to go. Your spirit temporarily drifts away from your body. This may already have happened to you at some time without you fully realising what was going on. You may have had the feeling that you were here, but not here; that part of you was somewhere else and in different surroundings, witnessing a different pocket of life, all in the space of a brief few moments. You cannot stay away too long because your energy level is dropping all the time. But you can travel anywhere.

I know, I've done it, but I don't do it very often because it's so exhausting. I love mountains and I have sometimes gone off to look down on some mountains. It is a marvellous feeling. You come back tired but refreshed.

An extraordinary thing happened to me many years ago which I still don't understand, but which I know was important. I drifted off on the astral plane, leaving my body and I didn't know if I was asleep or awake. I knew I had to go to a special place and I was flying over mountains until I came to one particular mountain where I saw three men standing on the mountainside. They were all dressed the same, in long shifts, each with a girdle around his waist and wearing sandals with no socks on. I wasn't sure why I was there but it felt as though I had to be given instructions about something.

I was standing on the mountainside and the eldest of the three, the man in the middle, was talking to me. I looked down beside me and there was a pretty little plant which I didn't recognise, I'd never seen one like it before. It had a tiny stem and pretty little leaves growing perfectly symetrically out of each side.

You know how sometimes, when you're talking, you fiddle with things near to hand or maybe you doodle. Well, as they talked, I was fiddling with this plant and picked a stem.

The old man finished giving me instructions and the next thing I knew was that I was back in bed again. Was it a dream? I don't think so, because, when I opened my hand, there was the stem and leaves of the plant I had picked.

I have never been able to remember what my instructions were – I don't think I even understood them at the time. They were put into my subconscious. But somehow I know that whatever I was instructed to do, whatever these instructions were, I have carried them out so far.

I can quite understand if all this sounds a bit silly to you and I don't expect people to believe me – it's a lot to take in. But I can assure you that it happened and I treasured that plant until, after many years, it fell to dust.

The more aware you become of your own psychic power the more you may want to use it. But now you have opened your mind you must learn to discipline your mind.

Clairvoyance, for example, is very hard work and very draining. You have to learn to concentrate your mind in one direction and that is not nearly as easy as it sounds. When your mind drifts off in completely the opposite direction – and it will, often – you have got to develop the discipline to bring it back to where you want it to focus.

You may be tempted to buy a crystal or some such thing advertised in psychic magazines. They can be helpful although all they are, as far as I'm concerned, is a prop; something for you to focus on, making disciplining your mind that much easier.

Psychometry, which means holding some object belonging to a person and then being able to pick up facts about their personality and their life from that object, is the same. It gives you something to focus on, it's a point of concentration. It isn't necessary, but it helps.

It is quite fun to practise using psychometry with the help of a friend. He or she presents you with an object, like a key or a piece of jewellery, and you try to pick up what you can from it. Don't try and be logical and rational about it and don't dismiss the first impressions that come into your mind even if they do not appear to make sense, because these are the ones that really matter.

Make sure your friend chooses an object that doesn't belong to him but to someone else – you know your friend too well and when you first start using your psychic power in psychometry you may be too tempted merely to repeat all that you already know about your friend!

A lot of these psychic games can be beneficial, and fun too, and they are quite harmless – as long as you don't start using uija boards or anything dangerous like that.

A favourite is the old mind-reading game. You and a friend sit with a piece of paper and a pen each. You ask your friend to draw a shape on his piece of paper (while you avert your eyes so you don't cheat by watching how the pen is moving!) Then you ask him to concentrate on that shape very hard. You concentrate too – on him – and draw the first shape that comes into your mind. To begin with the shape shouldn't be too complicated; maybe a square, a circle, a flower or doodle of a house – not the Forth Bridge! You will be amazed at the results you can get from games like this. It's entertaining, it's good practice and it helps you to discipline your mind.

But, of course, these are only games. The most important thing, the only true way to make the most of your own psychic gift, is to open your eyes, open your heart and your mind and change your attitude to the world in which you live. Once you do, I don't exaggerate when I say that you will be astounded at what you discover – not only about yourself but about life in this dimension. There are no boundaries, as with your psychic eye, you will see.

TEN

The Road Ahead

Lean on Me

Lean on me when heavy troubles touch your worried brow,
And I'll find the strength to carry you through God's grace
    somehow.
Perhaps a word, a smile, a prayer, or the touch of a loving
    hand,
These thoughts are deep within my soul, you may never
    understand.
And on my earthly journey this love I truly give,
To any one who is in need of the will to fight and live.
My oh so lonely mission so soon I must embark,
God gave to me a candle like a respite in the dark.
Oh, that I could but once enjoy that wondrous burning
    flame,
But I must go with silent tears on my lonely road again.
Although I walk in shadows and softly cry alone,
I pray God lights one candle that I may call my own.

A POEM FOR JACOB,
the most wonderful man I have ever known,
with thanks,
NELLA JONES, 1992

As the jumbo jet slowly taxied to a halt I rubbed at the tiny porthole window next to me, pressed my nose against it and peered out, anxious to catch my first sight of Japan.

I could just about see the Japanese television crew who had invited me to their country to help them, and their police force, get to the bottom of several unsolved crimes.

They had told me they would be filming my arrival so could I please remember to smile and wave as I left the plane. But nothing had prepared me for the reception I actually received.

I was exhausted after the long flight and I was so excited at the prospect of my first real trip abroad that I hadn't slept for a week! My dress was crumpled, my eyes red and my hair refused to lie down but, as I walked out onto the top of the aircraft steps, I felt like a real celebrity!

The TV lights almost blinded me but I could still make out the crowd of cheering people who had turned out to welcome me. It was a wonderful moment. Thrilling!

I was whisked off to a luxury hotel and all the time I was pinching myself. I couldn't believe this was happening to Nella Jones from Bexleyheath!

I stayed in Japan for three weeks. It was fascinating, but it was all go; up at eight and sometimes working until nearly midnight. The television people wanted to film me as I worked and they presented me with several unsolved cases. Most of them were very sad and, as always, following my psychic clues turned out to be a highly emotional experience for me.

The case that most sticks in my mind is that of a little boy who was only three when he went missing, a year before I arrived in Japan. He had been playing in the street one day with some of his friends when he was knocked down by a car. The driver was about to speed off until he realised someone had seen what he had done. So he went back, picked up the boy and told the eye witness he was taking the child to hospital. The little boy was never seen again.

I met the little boy's parents and, sitting amongst their son's toys, we wept together. I knew he was dead and I think they knew it too.

I knew that the best I could do for them was to find their little boy's grave and, after following a series of clues, I was able to lead the television people to a dirt road where I believed he had been buried under pipes that had been laid there a year before.

The television crew hired a mechanical digger and started to excavate. When he disappeared the little boy was wearing blue and white shoes and, suddenly, there was a little blue and white shoe amongst the pile of earth that the digger was spilling onto the ground.

Thousands of viewers saw it on television and the TV station's switchboard was jammed for hours by viewers phoning in to say what they had seen. I knew I was at the right place but the digging had to stop because of the pipes underneath. Yet I still hope that it was of some comfort to the parents to know where their child had been laid to rest.

There were other cases, including one involving a little girl who had been murdered, and the entire experience was emotionally gruelling. But I still had time to see the sights, to wander around and bask in the calm of the ancient Japanese temples, to soak up the life and culture of a country so different to ours and to meet the Japanese people who were consistently courteous and friendly.

By my last night I was quite a celebrity as so many people had seen me on television, and as a result I was guest of honour at a wonderfully lavish reception. I drank *saki* for the first time, watched Geisha Girls dancing and thoroughly enjoyed myself, while at the back of my mind I couldn't help thinking, 'Not bad for a South London charlady!'

Looking back, that trip to Japan fourteen years ago was one of the highlights of my life. I have always longed to travel and, apart from a couple of day trips to France, that was all I had done.

But then, I tell myself, I have probably met more people, people of all nationalities and from all walks of life, than anyone else I know. I have met the high and mighty, the popular and the poor. I have seen tremendous courage and goodness as well as, on occasions, tremendous evil.

I suppose I have achieved a lot in my life. I didn't climb out of the gutter, I literally clawed my way out and it was damned hard work. But at least I have the satisfaction of knowing that I did it all myself.

I have my house in Bexleyheath and, more than that, I have wonderful friends and I am blessed with a loving family.

Sadly, both my parents are now dead. Mum died over twenty years ago and my father just two years later. We had our troubles as a family when I was young but, in the later years, we were close and saw each other regularly. My brothers and sisters are all fit and well and live near me in Kent. And then there are the children.

When the boys were taken from me as children there followed the bleakest years of my life, years I prefer not to remember even now. Eric was just nine and Peter seven when they were taken away to boarding school. For six years we kept in touch by letter and phone calls and I saw them only during the school holidays. But, as soon as they were old enough to leave school, they came back to me and we have been a happy family ever since.

Eric is now 38 and a carpenter. He lives in Norfolk, with his lovely wife Carol, and just twenty miles up the road from him lives my younger son Peter, who is now 36. He's married to a sweet girl called Ursula and they have two children Ian, 15 and Isabel, 12.

Gaynor, my beautiful daughter, has grown up to be psychic like her mum. I suspected it when she was a small child, but I was sure of it when she was about ten years old. One night she crept into my bed sobbing. I was due to travel to London the next day but she pleaded with me not to go.

'All those poor people on the underground,' she cried. 'You mustn't go to London.'

The following day, February 28, 1975, was the date of one of London's worst train crashes, the Moorgate tube disaster.

Gaynor is now 26 and she has chosen not to use her psychic gift as I have done, but we both know it is there. It is there for her to bring out when she chooses to, it is there waiting for her. Maybe some time in the future she will follow in my footsteps, I cannot be sure.

In the meantime she is happily married to Karl and she is kept busy enough looking after my other two grandchildren, seven-year-old James and four-year-old Katie who are both a delight.

Of everything I have done in my life bringing Eric, Peter and Gaynor into the world has been my greatest achievement. I know all mums are incredibly proud of their children but all three of mine are very special to me. They keep me going and I don't know what I would have done without their love and support.

There is no special man in my life now. There was Eric and Ben and I spent fourteen years with a man called Albert. When I was fourteen he was my childhood sweetheart in Eynsford. He emigrated to Australia and we were reunited when he returned to England many years later. But sadly, that too didn't last.

Our parting was very painful. I haven't had much luck with the men in my life but, I have to be honest and say that being involved with someone like me can't be easy. If someone is in trouble, if someone is sick, I cannot turn them away. I simply cannot do it.

Much of my life is not my own and I think that sometimes, understandably, that can put a man's nose out of joint if, as most men do, he thinks he should be getting most of the attention! And then, of course, there is also the fact that many men might find it a bit intimidating to live with a woman who knows, or could know if she concentrated hard enough, what they were up to 24 hours of every day! Any fibs are simply out of the question when you are living with a psychic!

In many ways I hope Gaynor does not follow me and actively use her psychic gift. I say that, not only because I myself have had a hard life, but also because some of the things I see can be so deeply depressing.

In recent months I have been getting many visions, snatches of pictures that come and go, of the future that awaits us all – and much of it is hard to face.

I am still very concerned about the situation in the Middle East. Despite the victory of the allied forces in the Gulf War I can see that the trouble with Iraq is far from over yet.

I believed the allied forces made a grave mistake when they chose to halt the Gulf War when they did. We may well all pay for that in the next few years. I see much conflict in the Middle East. I am convinced that Saddam Hussein does have a nuclear weapon and that, worse still, at some time in the not too distant future he will use it.

I also see much conflict in Germany in the next three years. The growing strength of ultra-right wing parties will be an increasing cause for concern in Germany and the rise of fascist movements will not be confined to that country alone. Like the rest of Europe we will have our problems with right wing organisations here too, and it is going to take a lot of hard work to maintain peace on the streets when that happens.

I am afraid of little in this life but one thing that does frighten the living daylights out of me is extremes in the weather. For a quite long time now I have been seeing a change in the weather pattern which will affect us all in Britain.

Within the next few years here, in Europe and in the Middle East we will witness freak weather conditions, sudden extremes of weather we have never seen before. I can't even see whether it is extremes of heat or cold, wind or rain, but it will literally shock and shake us to our bones.

I think this could start very soon – maybe even within the next year – and, at the same time, I see a terrible earthquake in Japan. I see many hundreds of people dead and I can feel the fear, for I am sure there will be several smaller earthquakes over a wide area in that part of the world, maybe even stretching as far south as Australia.

Worldwide, I see alarm, in a couple of years' time, when people suddenly realise the full extent of the AIDS epidemic.

I have seen this plague coming for many, many years and I simply do not believe the authorities are telling us the whole story of how serious it is, in case it causes panic. As a result, people are complacent. In a few years' time, when their friends, family and nextdoor neighbours begin to die around them, only then will people wake up to the gravity of the situation. I also believe that, at the same time, it will be realised that condoms are not a sure protection against the disease.

Recently, I have seen a ship in trouble in the Channel just off the South Coast of England. The pictures are hazy. I know many will die but I cannot be sure where the ship is sailing from, or to. The feelings have been getting stronger so maybe this is a tragedy which will hit us soon, in the next year or so. Maybe, as we move nearer in time to the event, my pictures will become clearer. I hope so.

But it is not all bad news. I am really quite optimistic about the future of our country in the next ten years. Of course we will have our problems, especially, as I have said, with the far-right political groups who may cause unrest on our streets; but I think we have much to look forward to.

I believe there will be enormous changes in our way of life but most will be for the good. Repeatedly I have a strange feeling that I cannot explain. I am being told that things will be 'thinned out'. I am not sure exactly what this means but I have the feeling that somehow, before we enter the next century, we will have more space, more air to breathe.

Perhaps this means that finally those in power will devote more of their energy to tackling the problems of pollution. I am not sure. Whatever this thinning-out means, I can see an enormous shake-up in our system of transport within the next ten years. Travelling will be easier although, again, I am not sure why. I see roads emptier than they are now.

One thing I see over the next ten years, which pleases me enormously, is a change in people's attitudes towards psychic phenomena and people's own psychic powers. I am sure that the sixth sense will be proved scientifically and that this will happen soon, within the next three years.

Far into the future I see a very different world. The old order will change completely, the old structures will go. It is already beginning to happen. In Russia and elsewhere we are seeing the break-up of superpowers into smaller independent states and this trend will continue worldwide.

Many people talk these days about, or against, a United States of Europe but eventually there will be a kind of United States of the World with a central organisation, similar although not exactly the same as the United Nations. This will not happen in my lifetime, and maybe not in yours, but, believe me, it will happen.

As for me, I have my dreams like everyone else. I dream of travelling, especially to Morocco and Ireland, although I am not sure why those countries are important to me. And I dream of returning home to a country cottage where I will have a beautiful garden and grow my own vegetables. I will spend my days making jams and pickles, painting, writing.

But I fear that the picture is probably only a fantasy, never to be. I have known since I was very young that this is the path I had to take in this life. Everything that went before – my early years, all the different jobs, the sorrows, the struggles – were all just to prepare me for the time when I would use my gift to the full to help other people.

I am often very tired, my health is weak and I have no personal life to speak of. My life belongs to other people. When I am feeling down I think, 'When does my life begin? When do I get to do the things I want to do?' There never seems to have been any time to myself and there never seems to have been the money either!

But I know I have helped thousands of people and that is how I find my happiness – through the happiness of others. You can't imagine how rewarding it is when you meet someone who is sick and suffering, and then watch them leave, healed and with a lighter heart, knowing that you have helped them.

I still get the 'lonely feeling' but I have grown used to it by now. The 'lonely feeling' is part of me and I have learned to accept that no one has any idea how I feel deep inside, how my gift dictates my life.

I recently went back to the village of Eynsford where I grew up. It is as pretty as ever and I walked along the High Street to the bridge.

My initials, NS, are still there, still strong and deep, so there's a lot of life left in the old girl yet! And I still have work to do. So I press on and do my best. That's all any of us can do, isn't it?

We all have our own path to follow. I hope yours brings you happiness and I hope that, by using your psychic eye along the way, you will find fulfilment too.

God bless.

Nella.

Index